ROMAN CAMPS
IN BRITAIN ·

To Susan Walker
Thank you for teaching
one of the dedicatees of
this book how to read and
write!
Rebecca xx

ROMAN CAMPS
IN BRITAIN

REBECCA H. JONES

Rebecca H Jones

AMBERLEY

For Simon, Caitlin and Ryan

First published 2012

Amberley Publishing
The Hill, Stroud
Gloucestershire, GL5 4EP

www.amberleybooks.com

Copyright © Rebecca H. Jones, 2012

The right of Rebecca H. Jones to be identified as the Author
of this work has been asserted in accordance with the
Copyrights, Designs and Patents Act 1988.

British Library Cataloguing in Publication Data.
A catalogue record for this book is available from the British Library.

ISBN 978 1 84868 688 5

Typesetting and Origination by Amberley Publishing.
Printed in Great Britain.

Contents

Acknowledgements

I am grateful to the numerous colleagues who have, over the years, offered advice and support for my research on Roman camps. In particular, I would like to thank Professor Bill Hanson for suggesting this volume and supervising my work on Scotland, and Dr Jeffrey Davies for his advice and introducing me to Welsh camps. Humphrey Welfare and the late Dr Vivien Swan have always been tremendously helpful when looking at camps in England. I would also like to thank colleagues from the Roman Northern Frontier Seminars and the International Congresses of Roman Frontier Studies for many discussions on camps. I would especially like to thank Gordon Maxwell, Professor David Breeze, the late David Wilson, Professor Val Maxfield, Dr Fraser Hunter, Dr Jan Rajtar, Dr Claus-Michael Hüssen, Professor Ian Haynes and Dr Alan Leslie.

Professor David Breeze, Humphrey Welfare, Dr Jeffrey Davies and Dr Simon Gilmour all commented on earlier drafts of the text but any errors and views expressed are my own.

I must also thank numerous colleagues across Britain for information about their excavations on Roman camps, especially Murray Cook for discussions about his extensive excavations at Kintore, which have revolutionised our understanding of these structures.

Colleagues within the Royal Commission on the Ancient and Historical Monuments of Scotland have helped with fieldwork and interpretation of the results of ground and aerial survey, and kindly supplied the majority of the air photographs and some of the drawings in this book. Drawings of Welsh camps were made by Charles Green (for Davies and Jones 2006) and those of Scottish camps and maps by Kevin Hicks and Shelly Werner of CFA Archaeology (for Jones forthcoming 2011). I would also like to thank Peter Horne from English Heritage for kindly providing Plate 9, Professor Norman McCord and Newcastle University for Figure 28, AOC Archaeology Group for providing Figure 53, Professor David Breeze and Angus Lamb for Figure 13, English Heritage for Figure 66, and the staff of the Royal Commission on the Ancient and Historical Monuments of Wales for Figures 10, 16, 67, 68 and Plate 8. I would also like to thank colleagues from the Frontiers of the Roman Empire Culture 2000 project for the production of Plate 1, and Drs George Findlater and Simon Gilmour for being models for Plates 6 and 10.

Finally, I must thank my husband, Simon, and children Caitlin and Ryan, for tolerating my unhealthy interest in Roman camps.

Preface

This book is intended as a general introduction to the study of Roman temporary camps in Britain and much of the information and thoughts have been derived from three volumes on Roman camps in the three modern-day countries that make up the Roman province of Britannia. In 1995, Humphrey Welfare and the late Dr Vivien Swan produced a magisterial volume on the field archaeology of Roman camps in England, accompanied by a comprehensive gazetteer with plans based on detailed topographic survey and mapping of information available from air photographs. In 1999–2000, the present author was fortunate enough to spend a year working with Dr Jeffrey Davies at Aberystwyth University on a comparative volume for Wales which was published in 2006. This volume looked at the archaeology of Roman camps in Wales and the Marches and was accompanied by a gazetteer. The final volume of the trio, *Roman camps in Scotland*, written by this author, will be published in 2011 by the Society of Antiquaries of Scotland and includes a discussion of the archaeology and gazetteer of all known camps in Scotland. This volume was based on my PhD research at the University of Glasgow (awarded in 2006); I am grateful to my supervisor, Professor Bill Hanson, for his support in the final volume and for suggesting this introductory volume on Roman camps in Britain to Amberley Publishing. It seemed an appropriate time to produce an overall book on Roman camps in Britain and it is hoped that this volume provides a useful introduction to the subject – further reading is provided at the back, but for further information about the sites highlighted in the text, the reader is directed to the three volumes for England, Wales and Scotland, which have detailed descriptions and plans of all the sites and details of where to find further information for each of these. Many of the primary sources of information (original excavation reports) have not been quoted in detail here, but can be tracked down through these three books:

Welfare, H. and Swan, V. 1995. *Roman Camps in England. The Field Archaeology*. RCHME, London.

Davies, J. L. and Jones, R. H. 2006. *Roman Camps in Wales and the Marches*. University of Wales Press, Cardiff.

Jones, R. H. forthcoming 2011. *Roman Camps in Scotland*. Society of Antiquaries of Scotland, Edinburgh.

In addition, on-line national and local databases for the three countries can provide up-to-date information about individual sites. For the national records, the user is directed to PastScape and the Heritage Gateway for England (www.pastscape.org.uk and www.heritagegateway.org.uk), Coflein for Wales (www.coflein.gov.uk) and Canmore for Scotland (http://canmore.rcahms.gov.uk), along with numerous local online Sites and Monuments and Historic Environment Records, often (but not exclusively) held by heritage services in local authorities. The Ordnance Survey regularly produces revisions of its *Map of Roman Britain* (currently in its fifth edition, 2001), which includes the locations of all known camps.

1

Introduction

The Roman Empire was one of the greatest empires of the ancient world. It gradually grew in size from Rome and Italy to occupy not only a large part of modern day Europe but also parts of Asia, the near East and northern Africa (Plate 1)[1]. Expanding and maintaining that Empire required military might, and the Roman army was one of the most professional, organised and tactically skilled fighting forces that the world had ever seen. That army developed from one comprising Roman citizens (an expanding population as the Roman Republic and then Empire grew) organised ultimately into legions, to a more professional army that also incorporated and utilised local allied soldiers (*auxilia*) who supported the legions with additional fighting skills and knowledge, and particularly in the provision of cavalry. Eventually the army comprised a wide variety of men from a large geographic area and range of backgrounds – from senatorial rank to the poorest in society. Both in peacetime and at war, these men became highly trained and disciplined and were housed within the same fortifications – fortresses, forts and camps – although with differing living conditions according to rank. These forces could be extremely large; for example, it is estimated that Agricola, Roman governor of Britain in the later part of the first century, had about 21,000 men with him at the battle of Mons Graupius against the Caledonian tribes in AD 83 (see Chapter 5).

Considerable research – including survey and excavation – has been undertaken on Roman frontiers, fortresses and forts, and we now know a considerable amount about the life of the Roman soldier stationed in these fortifications. Although much is still to know, and every piece of research almost inevitably leads to tantalising new questions, they have been the subject of detailed study for a long period of time. Roman camps, the subject of this book, are one of the bridesmaids of the study of the fortifications of the Roman army, and were the most basic form of accommodation, occupied for a very limited period of time (and usually therefore referred to as 'temporary camps'). When the Romans invaded new territory they undertook certain standard activities; arriving at a new location for an overnight stop, they went about the business of laying out a fortified enclosure (often comprising a perimeter rampart and ditch) in which they, and all their baggage, animals and wagons, would camp. Depending on the size of the army, these enclosures could occupy considerable space, and the soldiers needed to find suitable large areas of ground on which to camp. Ancient writers on the techniques for setting out camps tell us that they should be built in safe places, not near areas where an enemy could hide (such as near a forest or gully) and close to where there were sufficient supplies of firewood, fodder and water. Certainly the availability of clean water was a priority. Such camp sites could be occupied for several days or weeks before the army moved on, potentially leaving the ground sullied by rubbish and latrine pits.

Although only occupied for a short period, a number of camp sites have survived the ravages of time to tell us something of the movements and activities of the Roman army in provinces around the Empire. While their remains may seem ephemeral when compared to some of the more dramatic Roman monuments that have survived today – frontier defences such as Hadrian's Wall, the Antonine Wall and the German *limes*, forts and fortresses (many built using stone) – nonetheless they paint an important picture of the Roman army and they are remarkable survivals in their own right. They can start to reveal details of the way in which Rome went about its campaigns and training regimes across the Empire, and also yield enticing clues about the daily lives of soldiers on the move.

Temporary Roman camp sites have now been recorded the length and breadth of the Roman Empire, from arable fields in north-eastern Scotland to desert frontiers in Jordan, from the mountains of Romania to the Rhine delta in the Netherlands. Some of the more famous examples are the siege camps surrounding the Jewish fortress at Masada in Israel (Figure 1), and those around the Celtiberian settlement of Numantia in northern Spain. But the area with the largest number of recognised camps is that of the island of Britain, with nearly 500 now known. There are a number of reasons for this, including our long tradition of recognition of such sites in the field, particularly from the eighteenth century onwards, the application of aerial survey to archaeology since the 1930s by pioneers with Roman interests (Chapter 6), and land management regimes particular to the United Kingdom. In recent years, the expansion of aerial survey and photography programmes in other countries on the frontiers of the Roman Empire has identified new camps, with both Slovakia and the Czech Republic seeing a recent explosion of discoveries. Britain has also benefited from the recent survey, research, excavation and publication of its camps in books discussing the archaeology of camps (with comprehensive gazetteers and plans) for England and Wales, with the publication of the volume for Scotland in 2011[2].

The Roman period in Britain benefits from a strong tradition of archaeological research combined with classical literature which gives details about particular episodes in history. Other forms of written archaeological evidence – including coins, inscriptions on stone and other objects (for example, pottery) and the ink writing tablets from the Roman fort of Vindolanda on Hadrian's Wall[3] – add further details. There are numerous summaries of sources in general texts on the Romans in Britain as well as an overview source book[4] and detailed lists of Roman inscriptions[5]. Although archaeology and history should be complementary to one another, we must always acknowledge the biases of the authors composing the texts and the assumptions that we make regarding archaeological data – at times archaeology has been used to confirm historical statements, or classical sources plundered to help understand the archaeology – not always with success. The first half of this book commences with a brief general overview of the Roman conquest of Britain, primarily from literary sources with some archaeology (Chapter 2). In Chapter 3, I explain what Roman camps were used for and divide the archaeological remains into potential functional

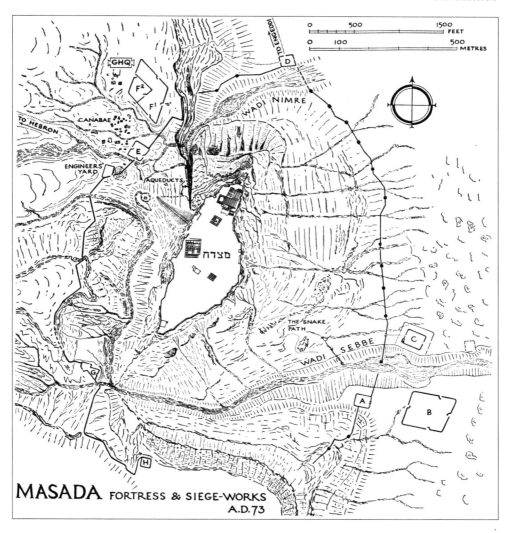

1. Plan of the camps and siege works at Masada, Israel, made by Ian Richmond in 1960. (Reproduced from the *Journal of Roman Studies* 1962)

categories, using archaeology and literature. This is followed by a chapter on historical sources, ranging from military manuals through to the histories and biographies that tell us about the activities of Roman forces in the field as well as more specific information about their actions in Britain. Chapter 5 assesses the information that the classical sources provide with regard to the layout, orientation and holding capacity of camps, coupled with examples from the archaeological record in Britain, accepting that some of these exercises, particularly with regard to holding capacity, are highly speculative and must be treated as hypothetical case studies.

The second half of the book focuses on the archaeology of Roman camps in Britain, commencing with an explanation of how we know what we know, through the research of antiquarian scholars, pioneers of aerial survey for archaeology and the potential that remote sensing now offers. Chapter 7 looks at the re-use and survival of these structures, both in the Roman period and later, and the ways in which some have survived. In Chapter 8, I provide a more detailed discussion of our archaeological knowledge of the features recorded for temporary camps – their perimeter defences, entrance protection, their morphological shapes, annexes and internal features including ovens and pits, many of which have been found through excavations, with a case study discussion of the evidence from the relatively recent extensive excavations at Kintore in Aberdeenshire, which have helped to revolutionise our understanding of the Roman army on the move and in camp. The following chapter looks at the distribution of camps and how our archaeological understanding can help interpret their chronology and context. Finally, in the concluding chapter, I surmise potential chronologies of the use of camps in Britain, based on the currently available evidence outlined in the preceding chapters.

2

The Roman Conquest of Britain

The history of the Roman conquest of Britain is well documented and fuller descriptions are available in numerous publications. Even so, much of our knowledge is derived from historical sources, sometimes married with archaeological evidence, none of which provides a full detailed account. However, they do shine a spotlight on our understanding of certain parts of Britain at specific points in time.

On the eve of the Roman conquest of Britain, classical sources knew that Britain was an island and compared the lifestyle of the indigenous Britons to those of Gaul (modern-day France), about whom the Romans were hearing much thanks to Julius Caesar's conquests of Gaul in the 50s BC and his descriptive accounts[1]. Caesar described the Britons as following a pastoral rather than arable way of life and dyeing their skin blue with woad[2]. The island was also described as thickly wooded by the Greek geographer Strabo, writing in the late first century BC/early first century AD[3]. Both of these descriptions we know to be exaggerated – archaeological environmental evidence indicates that large parts of the landscape was cleared of trees from the Neolithic period onwards, long before the arrival of the Romans, and that arable agriculture was practiced. Iron Age communities lived in both nucleated and dispersed roundhouse settlements which were often enclosed by ramparts and ditches and came together into tribal groupings.

The presence of the Romans in northern Gaul brought them into much closer contact with Britain. Caesar claimed that Britons had supported Rome's enemies during his conquest of Gaul, which gave him the excuse to cross the Channel and invade, supported by envoys from some of the tribes of southern Britain who suggested that they would submit to the authority of Rome. Julius Caesar mounted two expeditions to Britain in the summers of 55 and 54 BC, establishing a beach head camp which has not been located but is believed to have been in Kent. Caesar's own propagandist writings suggested that he had been victorious and chose not to pursue a conquest of Britain. In the words of the Roman historian Tacitus, writing in the late first/early second century AD: '[Caesar] can be considered to have pointed it [Britain] out, not handed it over, to future generations.'[4] Certainly, Caesar bequeathed an increase in trade and diplomacy between the Roman occupied continent and the island of Britain.

It was almost a century later, in AD 43, when a full invasion force arrived, led by Aulus Plautius under the orders of the Emperor Claudius. Using the pretext of resolving tribal disputes between some of the southern kings, but also in need of a victory to consolidate his newly acquired position as emperor, the literary sources tell us that Claudius briefly joined Plautius in order to claim the triumph. The landing point of the invasion force is unknown, with arguments made for both Richborough in Kent and Fishbourne near Chichester in Sussex. Archaeology has yet to provide enough detailed evidence to support either claim.

The conquest of Britain gradually expanded from south-east England to the north and west, but was not a straightforward process. Thanks to the late first/early second-century AD Roman historian and biographer Gaius Suetonius, we know that the later Emperor Vespasian (AD 69–79 and founder of the late first-century Flavian dynasty) was commander of the *legio II Augusta* during the initial Claudian conquest and actively campaigned in south-west England, fighting 'thirty battles, subjugating two warlike tribes and capturing more than twenty towns'[5] (probably hill-forts). Another historian (Tacitus, see Chapter 4) tells us that Ostorius Scapula, governor from AD 47–51, established forts to hold the country between the Trent and the Severn[6]. Caratacus of the Catuvellauni tribe (based around St Albans in Hertfordshire), one of the leaders of the resistance to the Roman occupation, fled to help the Silures and Ordovices in Wales[7] following conquest of the lands of the Catuvellauni. After a battle with the Romans in AD 51, Caratacus fled to the Brigantes (in northern England) but was handed over by them as a prisoner to the Roman governor.

Despite the defeat of Caratacus and his followers, it still took the best part of thirty years until the area now known as Wales was conquered and garrisoned. In AD 60, we are informed that the governor, Suetonius Paullinus, was attacking Mona (Anglesey), but his campaigns were cut short by the revolt of Boudica and her followers in eastern England and the army marched back to the south-east to deal with this rebellion. Despite pockets of resistance in southern England, the tribes of Wales clearly represented a significant area of stubborn, long-term resistance to Rome, no doubt aided and abetted by their substantial upland terrain. Campaigns here continued, albeit intermittently, until AD 77 when we are told that Julius Frontinus, governor of Britain (AD 73/4–77), subjugated the Silures[8] and his successor, Julius Agricola (AD 77–83), suppressed a rebellion of the Ordovices, who had nearly wiped out a cavalry regiment stationed in their territory[9]. Agricola is reported as taking swift action and also re-conquering Anglesey.

During this period also, the Romans encountered resistance in northern England. Instability in the Empire in AD 68–9 (the 'Year of Four Emperors') provided an ideal opportunity for the Brigantes to mount serious hostilities against the Roman presence, and it seems apparent from the sources and the archaeological remains that this area was a priority for the two governors in the period AD 69–74, Vettius Bolanus (AD 69–71) and Petillius Cerealis (AD 71–4). Timbers found at the Roman fort at Carlisle have been dated to AD 72/3 and it therefore seems likely that Cerealis was also campaigning in southern Scotland by this period.

For the period AD 77–83 we are fortunate to have Tacitus' detailed biography of Agricola (see Chapter 4). While such an apparently detailed literary source can aid the consideration of archaeological evidence, care must be taken not to impose the history on the archaeology. Many of Tacitus' contemporaries would have known about the period about which he was writing and there must be a significant amount of fact contained in this narrative, but Britain was far from the streets of Rome and Tacitus had his own reasons to glorify

Agricola, including his own familial connections and a desire to honour his father-in-law after the death of the despotic Emperor Domitian (who was assassinated in AD 96). We must therefore be careful in interpreting this evidence in conjunction with archaeological information.

Nonetheless, the text of the *Agricola* has been used by many scholars to tell the story of the conquest of Scotland, and it does add a significant amount to the archaeological evidence, although the reality was undoubtedly more complex. Some of the first-century AD military remains in Scotland probably date from Agricola's predecessors as well as to the period after his recall from Britain. In his seventh and final season, Tacitus states that Agricola defeated the Caledonians at the battle of Mons Graupius[10], but the site of this battle has not been identified, and remains a subject of fascination and speculation. Many antiquarians used Tacitus to try to construct a geography of Roman Scotland and identify the battle site, but to no avail, and the search for the battle has not lost its appeal to current generations. Numerous locations have been put forward with differing degrees of credibility, ranging from southern Perthshire to Inverness and even further north, studying place names and archaeological evidence, although not all sites proposed appeared to have Roman origins[11]. Indeed, one claim favours a location at Dunning in southern Perthshire, close to the site of the later Pictish Battle of Duncrub (*c.* AD 964)[12]. Although studies of language and place names provide supporting evidence to this claim, the archaeological evidence is tenuous at best, and the assertion of this location remains speculative. It is also believed that the root of the word 'Graupius' is the same root as that for the Grampian mountains, but that only serves to slightly narrow the likely geography. Another favoured location is the landscape between the extremely large Roman camp at Logie Durno in Aberdeenshire and the hills of Bennachie, the highest of eastern Aberdeenshire (Plate 2). While a persuasive argument has been put forward for this location[13], there is, at present, no supporting evidence and discrepancies exist between the literary evidence and the physical geography. Even with the sophisticated detection techniques available now, the site remains elusive. Yet persistent research in Germany eventually did identify the location of the defeat of Publius Quinctilius Varus and three legions in the Teutoburg Forest in AD 9[14], keeping the hope that archaeological evidence may yet furnish clues to the battle site of Mons Graupius.

After the battle, Tacitus reports that Agricola sent the fleet on a circumnavigation of Britain which no doubt provided useful information to the occupying forces both in terms of the geography of the island as well as further information on Iron Age communities with whom Rome had thus far had limited contact. Certainly there are quite a number of Roman artefacts recorded from Iron Age settlements beyond the part of Britain that was conquered by the Romans[15]. For example, at the Broch of Gurness Iron Age stone settlement on the northern side of Mainland Orkney, sherds of Roman amphora (a vase-shaped storage container, possibly for wine) have been found of a type which date to pre-AD 60, suggesting potentially significant links between the elite members of Orcadian society and either the south of Britain or Rome. The historian Eutropius, writing in the latter half of the fourth century AD, claimed that the Orkneys were conquered under Claudius[16], but some form of contact rather than conquest is much more likely.

2. Distribution
map of known
and probable
camps in Britain.

Following the subjugation of the Caledonian tribes, Tacitus reports bitterly that Britain, having been conquered, was immediately thrown away[17], with the northern part of the province abandoned shortly afterwards. Changes of policy in Rome and pressures elsewhere in the Empire saw the abandonment of Scotland by about AD 105, and the establishment and consolidation of a series of forts along the Stanegate, the Roman road running across the Tyne–Solway isthmus. The Emperor Trajan (AD 98–117) is known for focusing his energies on the conquest of Dacia (modern day Romania) but there are references to soldiers stationed in Britain being decorated as a result of a British war[18] and when Hadrian became emperor in AD 117 (until AD 138), we are informed that the Britons could not be kept under Roman control[19] and the new emperor's response to this led to the construction of Hadrian's Wall in the AD 120s. Following Hadrian's death in AD 138, his successor Antoninus Pius ordered the re-conquest of lowland Scotland under Lollius Urbicus, governor of Britain, and the construction of a new frontier work, the Antonine Wall, across the Forth–Clyde isthmus. This frontier was provided with a series of outposts stretching up to Bertha near Perth. While there were undoubtedly also campaigns beyond the frontier, archaeology has not yet furnished us with any clear evidence to suggest how far north campaigning might have reached beyond the Tay.

By the early 160s, most Roman forces had once more left Scottish soil and returned to the line of Hadrian's Wall. There might have been trouble in south-west Scotland in the AD 150s which may have hastened the Roman retreat southwards. Classical texts suggest a level of unrest in Britain in the 160s and 170s, culminating in the crossing of a Wall (it is not stated which one but generally assumed to be Hadrian's) and the killing of a general, resulting in campaigns in the north by Ulpius Marcellus in the early 180s[20]. An inscription found at the fortress of Carpow on the Tay might date to the reign of the Emperor Commodus (AD 180–192)[21]. It is also reported that further trouble in the late 190s forced the governor Virius Lupus to buy off the northern tribes for a large sum[22]. Excavations at the Iron Age settlement at Birnie on the Moray Plain have uncovered two Roman coin hoards alongside numerous other Roman artefacts; the latest date from the coin hoards is AD 196, which fits into this historical context of a 'buy off' of the local tribes by Virius Lupus[23].

But the bribes appeared to have brought a relatively short period of quiet before we are told in around AD 207 that the barbarians were in revolt, looting the countryside and creating havoc[24]. This led to the next major recorded advance – the Severan re-conquest of the north, under the personal supervision of the Emperor Septimius Severus and his sons in AD 208–11. Severus apparently campaigned to the furthest point of the island[25], but any victory was not consolidated because, following the death of Severus in York in AD 211, his son Caracalla abandoned the northern conquests and returned to Rome.

In addition to the above, other literary sources also note campaigns by Constantius Chlorus into the territory of the 'Picts' in AD 305, that there was again trouble with the Picts in the AD 360s and possible Pictish wars in the AD 390s[26]. The Emperor Constans came over to Britain in AD 342–3 and this may have been in response to a military situation[27].

This very brief overview of the conquest of Britain, documented through literary sources and archaeological evidence, provides the context for our assessment of temporary camps. While difficult to date, temporary camps must fit into a historical framework of the conquest and occupation of the area in which they are found, which can be partially identified through the literary texts and detailed examination of the archaeological remains of Roman structures such as forts and fortresses. The distribution map of camps in Britain shows that the majority are known from recorded trouble spots: Wales, northern England and Scotland (Figure 2).

3
What is a Roman Camp?

Roman camps are temporary fortifications constructed by troops on campaigns or manoeuvres. Unlike constructions designed for more permanent occupation, these were usually occupied for only a few days or weeks and leave limited archaeological evidence, with no fixed internal structures. The better known forts and fortresses across the Empire contained buildings constructed in either timber or stone, including headquarters buildings (*principia*), the commanding officer's house (*praetorium*), barrack blocks for the soldiers (for soldiers and horses together in cavalry barracks), granaries (*horrea*), and sometimes workshops (*fabrica*), a bathhouse and latrine, a hospital (*valetudinarium*) and houses for the officers. Smaller fortifications, known as fortlets, usually contained accommodation for a limited number of men in barrack blocks. There were a number of roads running through a typical fort and around the inside of its perimeter, which was usually protected with an earth, turf or stone rampart with external ditch. Roman camps were based on a very similar model (and indeed it is probably more accurate to say that the layout of permanent forts copied that of earlier temporary structures such as camps), but they held leather tents instead of buildings and the perimeter defences, while still significant, are often smaller. It is possible that some forts started life as temporary camps, with shelters constructed over the tents when they were occupied for a longer period. This has been suggested elsewhere based on the interpretation of the archaeological remains of some of the forts constructed in Germany under the reign of the Emperor Augustus (27 BC – AD 14). In addition, at the Roman fort at Strageath in Perthshire, the excavators used the evidence of an early granary to suggest that it supplied the troops who were living in tents inside the fort while building its ramparts and gates[1]. This explanation seems eminently possible, because the troops building the fort need not necessarily require to occupy a different patch of land during its construction, although that is dependent on there being enough space for the number of troops to be quartered within the ramparts. While erecting a temporary camp would not have been overly time consuming to an army thoroughly trained in such matters, it might be more efficient for the troops to demarcate the area and build from within, assuming that there was sufficient space. It might be presumed that the presence of tents in the interior of the fort would be an obstacle when attempting to build internal structures. Yet troops could live in tents in one part of the fort while constructing their barracks in another, which might help to explain the lack of camps recorded in the vicinity of some forts across Britain.

Many of the camps recorded in Britain and around the Roman Empire are interpreted as marching or campaign camps, and were constructed by soldiers on active campaign away from their base through lands not yet conquered or fully held by the Romans. But other functions for temporary camps have also been identified, including siege camps, construction or labour camps, and practice camps.

MARCHING CAMPS

Marching or campaign camps were, as the name suggests, constructed by troops on the march or active campaign. But even within this general category it is clear from the wide range of sizes of marching camps that they held anything from small groups of troops perhaps on reconnaissance and scouting missions (the *exploratores*) gathering intelligence, to large armies intent on total conquest of new territories.

3. Aerial view of the marching camp at Forteviot in Perthshire, taken from the north in 1992. © Crown Copyright: RCAHMS. SC1164091. Licensor www.rcahms.gov.uk

One example of a marching camp is that at Forteviot in Perthshire, lying on a level terrace close to a meander in the River Earn (Figure 3). It has only been recorded through differential crop growth (crop-markings) seen on air photographs (see Chapter 6) but the majority of the perimeter ditch of the camp has been recorded, enabling us to record its large size (26 hectares/64 acres), identify a number of gates (probably six), and group it with other camps of a similar size (see Chapter 9). This camp probably held a large number of soldiers (perhaps in excess of 12,000 men – see Chapter 5) involved in campaigning or marching through Perthshire and Angus, the exact date of which is unknown.

SIEGE CAMPS

Siege camps are well attested in classical literature, with some of the most evocative descriptions surviving in Julius Caesar's descriptions of his Gallic Wars (particularly the siege of Alesia in France) and Josephus' descriptions of Rome's wars against the Jews (see Chapter 4). Indeed, remains of siege works are scattered throughout the Roman Empire, with some of the more famous examples being Numantia in Spain (Plate 3), Alesia in France, Masada in Israel (Figure 1) and Machaerus in Jordan[2]. Siege camps were sometimes, but not always, accompanied by a running breastwork or circumvallation (a line of fortifications which might encircle the subject to be besieged). In Britain, there are no confirmed siege camps although there are a number of disputed sites. Llanymynech Hill on the Montgomery/Shropshire border has been proposed as the site of the last stand of Caratacus and the Silures (a Iron Age tribe who occupied southern Wales) against Rome in AD 51 (also see Chapter 5) but this has not gathered general acceptance[3]. The earthworks on Woden Law in the Scottish Borders, once proposed as Roman training siege works, are now thought to be of Iron Age date[4]. The camps at Cawthorn in North Yorkshire have been referred to as practice siege camps but have now been reinterpreted as two forts and a camp[5].

The other site, still hotly disputed, is that of Burnswark Hill in Annandale, Dumfriesshire. Dominating the lands north of the Solway, and visible from the western end of Hadrian's Wall, lies the flat-topped hill of Burnswark (Figure 4)[6]. Spectacular views can be seen from its summit. The hill itself is crowned by an Iron Age hill-fort (which has been suggested as the *oppidum* – the main settlement – for the Novantae tribe), with an earlier Bronze Age cairn, later post-medieval artillery fortification (possibly a Civil War redoubt), and an Ordnance Survey triangulation station also recorded. The hill is flanked by two Roman camps, both of which exhibit unusual elements. The south camp is close in shape to the usual rectangular form often exhibited by camps (Chapter 8) but lies on quite sloping ground on the side of the hill and is bisected by a stream (known locally as 'Agricola's Well', after the famous first-century AD Roman Governor of Britain). Underneath its northern corner is a small rectangular earthwork enclosure, cut by platforms for later roundhouses. This enclosure has been traditionally interpreted as a Roman fortlet but recent re-assessment suggests that it may not be a Roman construction at all but related to Iron Age occupation.

The most unusual element of this camp is its gates (Figure 5). With central gates in its north-east, south-east and south-west sides, protected by additional stretches of ditch

4. Aerial view of Burnswark
Hill in Dumfriesshire, taken
from the north-east in 1990,
showing the hill and south
camp. © Crown Copyright:
RCAHMS. SC1164088.
Licensor www.rcahms.gov.uk

5. Aerial view of the gates
of Burnswark South camp
in Dumfriesshire, taken
from the north-west in
1990. © Crown Copyright:
RCAHMS. SC1234182.
Licensor www.rcahms.gov.uk

6. Aerial view of the North camp at Burnswark in Dumfriesshire, taken from the north-west in 1990. © Crown Copyright: RCAHMS. SC1164089. Licensor www.rcahms.gov.uk

(*tituli* – see Chapter 8), the camp appears normal, but its north-west side possesses three entrances, all protected by circular platforms (known as 'The Three Brethren') which are huge in size, measuring 3.5 m high and up to 15 m across. These have been interpreted as 'ballista platforms' or '*ballistaria*', firing ranges for Roman field-artillery[7]. This interpretation has been challenged, and an alternative view proposed that they were so designed to deflect heavy and destructive objects rolled towards the camp from the summit of the hill[8]. Excavations in the 1890s recorded that the ditch of one of these platforms was cut into rock and partially stone-faced; later excavations revealed that part of the ditch of the camp was cut through soft bedrock with stones also operating as a kerb to the rampart. The earlier excavations had also recorded that the rampart and ditch was stone faced; pavements were also recorded in the gateways and camp interior and a possible building in the centre of the camp but the later trenches failed to locate this structure, although an area of paving was noted.

The camp on the north side of the hill is a slightly unusual shape and gives the impression of two separate camps that have been joined together (Figure 6), although excavations in the 1950s failed to find supporting evidence. There is a gap in the rampart on its north-western side, due to boggy ground, and it is possible that an alternative means of protection was deployed for this stretch. The eastern part of the camp has three entrances with protective traverse ditches, and there is an odd entrance on its south-eastern side which appears to be protected by an additional stretch of rampart and ditch still attached to the camp, although the remains have been blurred by one of the trackways which run around the hill. Excavations in the 1890s recorded that the ditch was rock-cut in places; later excavations on the rampart in the 1960s noted that it comprised red clay standing on two or three courses of cut turf bricks.

The use of stone in parts of the south camp and the cutting ditch of both camps through rock in places represents a substantial amount of manpower for a site with temporary occupation and it is possible that the camps had prolonged occupancy or that a level of permanency in occupation was intended. However, because much of this evidence relies on the excavations in the 1890s which has not been confirmed through more limited later trenching, it is possible that some of the earlier findings may have been over-interpreted.

The trackways and field walls around the hill and below the hill-fort have been interpreted as lines of circumvallation, reinforcing the notion that the site was a Roman siege. Two further earthworks on the north-east and south sides of the hill were also interpreted as smaller Roman enclosures, but these are now believed to be prehistoric settlements[9] and the alleged line of circumvallation is not believed to be of Roman date. But this need not argue that the site was not one of a genuine siege. Some sieges utilised camps in a pincer movement on their target; for example, at Nahal Hever in Israel, two camps thought to date to the Bar-Kokhba War of *c.* AD 132–5 sit on either side of cliff edges, overlooking caves housing Jewish insurgents, with the two camps functioning to spy on and blockade the enemy[10]. At Corfinium in Italy, besieged by Caesar in 49 BC during the civil wars, two camps were constructed before work started on circumvallation[11]. It is possible that two camps were felt to be sufficient to take Burnswark hill, or that a circumvallation was intended but never constructed.

The hill has attracted considerable attention since the eighteenth century and the possibility that it was the site of a genuine siege gripped the imagination of many generations. Various Roman weapons including spear-heads, lead sling-bullets (*glandes*, possibly catapult ammunition), iron arrowheads and stone ballista balls have been found on the hill, broadly dating from the first to the second century AD. The interpretation of the site as that of a genuine Roman siege was questioned in the 1960s, with an alternative view put forward that it represented the remains of a practice siege by the Roman army, reinforced by excavations on the hill-fort in the 1960s and 1970s which suggested that the defences of the hill-fort were abandoned long before the Roman invasion and that the target for these weapons was stone paving laid out over an abandoned hill-fort gate. The view of this as a Roman army training area was reinforced by the earlier 1890s discoveries of paving and structures inside the south camp. It was proposed that the siege took place in the second century AD, and that some of the lead shot found on the fort was no longer in active use by this time and therefore represented use and disposal of earlier ammunition. The argument was also bolstered by the fact that the slopes of the hill are not particularly steep, although the geography need not mean that there was not a hostile community on the summit of the hill, which is the most prominent mound in the area. This view of a practice siege has been disputed more recently, the abandonment of the defences not necessarily meaning that there could not be a contemporary open settlement on the hill-fort, lying within the earlier ramparts which are still clearly visible today, and one of the round houses on the hill-fort may have been occupied in the second century AD (the dating reinforced through pottery recovered from the site).

The literary sources provide no further clues, and the date of the occupation of the camps remains uncertain. The site lies only 30 km north-west of Carlisle, where the earliest fort has been dated through waterlogged timbers to AD 72/3, and a Roman presence in south-west Scotland in the AD 70s seems highly likely. Troubles in the AD 150s have been proposed for south-west Scotland which may have led to a retreat from Scotland and re-occupation of Hadrian's Wall. Campaigns in the north under the governor Ulpius Marcellus in the AD 180s are also a possibility, as are the campaigns of the Emperor Severus in the early third century AD (see Chapter 5). Burnswark remains an enigmatic and controversial site.

CONSTRUCTION CAMPS

Construction or labour camps were those built to house troops engaged in the construction of a nearby fort, road or frontier. Although a straightforward definition, separating construction camps from the general mass of camps in Britain is fraught with difficulty. Proximity to fort, fortress or frontier need not mean that a camp housed troops involved in its construction. As noted earlier, the possibility exists that troops building a fort were housed in tents within the perimeter of the fort.

Glancing at a distribution of camps in Britain (Figure 2), it is clear that there was a preference for camping close to Roman roads and fort sites (whether sited in proximity to a later fort site, one demarcated for fortified occupation, or one already in use). Many of the lines of camps that can be seen in Figure 2 flank the routes of Roman roads and will represent marching camps. Use of the same routes for the subsequent construction of roads is hardly surprising, because these generally represent the best ways through territory as well as being good sites for halting for periods of time. The Romans made maps of conquered territory, probably in the form of Itineraries, and it was practical to re-use routes (particularly Roman roads) and return to existing fort sites (whether still occupied or not) to camp. In short, the placing of a camp beside a fort does not necessarily mean that the two are related. Further, the identification of construction camps is problematic because there was no standard size for these camps – this depended on the number of troops considered required or available for the building work.

The two frontier Walls in Britain, Hadrian's Wall and the Antonine Wall, are surrounded by a plethora of camps. Those along Hadrian's Wall exhibit a wide range of sizes, but commonality can be found among the camps along the Antonine Wall in Scotland. The majority of these are of a similar shape and size (2–2.5 ha/5–6 acres) and lie at relatively regular distances along the Wall (Figure 7).

The camps lying along the Antonine Wall have been recorded through differential crop-markings from the air since the 1940s. None survive as features discernable above ground although excavations have demonstrated the presence of substantial perimeter ditches, the features causing the crop-markings enabling the camps to be identified (see Chapter 6) (Plate 4). The Wall is also fortunate to have a series of distance slabs found which tell us which unit constructed how much of the Wall (Figure 8). The apparent standard size of the camps along the Wall (around 2 ha) suggests a standard garrison for the groups of legionary detachments charged with the construction of the frontier. In addition, there are four camps along the Wall which are approximately twice the size of the other camps, and are about 4.8 ha in size (12 acres). Two of these lie to the north of the Wall (Balmuildy and Wester Carmuirs, see Figure 7), which could indicate that they were early in the construction sequence for the Wall, potentially before or during the completion of the mural barrier in those sectors, because once the Wall was complete and in operation, any later troops would be more likely to camp in the secure area to the south of the frontier. They may relate to the construction of forts. One of these larger camps, Dullatur, was subject to excavations in the late 1990s which produced pottery dating to the late Hadrianic/early Antonine period, thereby indicating its contemporaneity with the construction of the Wall. Part of the perimeter of Dullatur was reused for a smaller camp, probably in the 2–2.5 ha range, although the full size of either camp is not known, only presumed from the known sides (Plate 5). Although this camp did not produce any additional dating

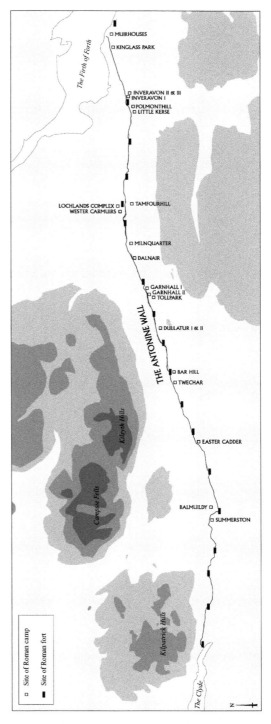

7. Map of the camps along the Antonine Wall. © Crown Copyright: RCAHMS. Licensor www. rcahms.gov.uk

8. Distance slab from Bridgeness, at the eastern end of the Antonine Wall. © Crown Copyright: RCAHMS. SC732497. Licensor www.rcahms.gov.uk

9. Aerial view of the camp at Steeds Stalls in Perthshire, showing the upstanding and crop-mark 'stalls', taken from the north-west in 1977. © Crown Copyright: RCAHMS. SC1164186. Licensor www.rcahms.gov.uk

evidence, it is likely that it too related to the construction of the Wall, which may have taken several years and was subject to a change of plan before construction was complete. This reinforces the suggestion that these larger camps were early in the construction sequence for the Wall, with the second camp required when further work was undertaken by a smaller number of men, either on the construction of the Wall or for later repairs[12].

Underneath the forts of Croy Hill and Bar Hill on the Antonine Wall lie two small additional structures that may have had a role in the construction sequence for the Wall. Excavations at Croy Hill suggest that the structure here dated to the Antonine period and it is possible that the feature at Bar Hill was also Antonine in date. Neither resemble camps known elsewhere, but both may have had a role early in the construction of the Wall: Bar Hill is sited close to the mid-point of the Wall at its highest point, and Croy Hill is close to the highest point on that hill; both have good views along the line of the Wall and to each other. It is possible that these two were construction camps of sorts, potentially housing teams of surveyors engaged in the initial planning of the frontier[13].

Another camp usually interpreted as having a role in construction is that at Steeds Stalls in Perthshire (Figure 9). This camp lies about 3 km north of the legionary fortress at Inchtuthil on the eastern part of the Hill of Gourdie. A Roman quarry has been recorded some 700 m away, and parts of a Roman road, possibly running from Inchtuthil to the quarry and Steeds Stalls, has also been identified. The camp is almost square in form, enclosing just over 2 ha (5 acres), a similar size to the camps along the Antonine Wall. Its perimeter is known only through crop-markings, with an unusual internal ditch dividing the interior into north and south. The site is named Steeds Stalls because of the presence of some upstanding remains in its northern half, referred to as 'stalls' and interpreted by antiquarians as the advance guard of the Caledonian army, sent to watch the Romans in their nearby fortress. These remains are accompanied by further crop-mark 'stalls' which have a tadpole-like appearance, with a round head some 4.5 m in diameter and a tail some 6 m in length leading out towards the camp perimeter. Similar 'tails' are also visible as crop-markings at the back of the upstanding stalls, and there may be some fourteen or fifteen 'stalls' in total. Although unexcavated, these features could be lime-kilns relating to the construction of the Inchtuthil fortress, thereby giving the site a likely interpretation as a construction camp[14]. Certainly, lime mortar was used extensively in the Roman world and guidelines for lime mortar mixes are provided in the writings of Vitruvius, a Roman architect and engineer writing in the first century BC[15].

PRACTICE CAMPS

Practice camps are the smallest category of Roman camp and were usually built in order for the soldiers to practice camp (and possibly fort) construction. Their size (most are smaller than 0.3 ha [⅔ acre] with many under 0.1 ha [¼ acre]) is a major factor in their identification and interpretation as practice camps, but they also display a concentration on the 'difficult' areas to be built: the entrances and rounded corners. They are usually known in clusters close to forts – presumably these are the 'parent' forts which housed the troops being trained. Quite a large number of these are now known in upland areas in

10. Aerial view of the practice camp at Braich-ddû in Merioneth, taken from the north-east in 2005. © Crown Copyright: Royal Commission on the Ancient and Historical Monuments of Wales. 2005.2967.

Wales, giving the impression that parts of that country operated as a Roman equivalent of Salisbury Plain[16]. Elsewhere in Britain there are other small camps, but few cluster in the same way as in Wales and, at the larger end of the spectrum, these camps could have held troops in tents. The smallest in Britain, Llyn Hiraethlyn IV in Merioneth, north Wales, is little more than 14 m square (see below; Figure 11); a nearby camp at Braich-ddû (also Merioneth) had such pronounced gate defences protruding into the interior that these left little or no room for the pitching of even a single tent (Figure 10).

The second-century AD author Appian, writing about the Spanish Wars of the second century BC, tells us a little of the training regimes demanded by Scipio Africanus the Younger: 'He marched all over the nearby plains and each day built and demolished a new camp, one after another, dug very deep ditches and filled them in, constructed high walls and overthrew them; he himself inspected everything from morning to night'[17]. This reference to filling the camps in after construction may be one reason why practice camps can be hard to find. But it is apparent that the protocol of demolishing a camp was not always practiced particularly, it seems, in Wales.

Four practice camps are recorded at Llyn Hiraethlyn, on a low plateau some 4 km along the Roman road from the Roman fort of Tomen-y-Mur in Snowdonia. Recorded through aerial survey and mapping in 1996, they are relatively well preserved and range in size from just over 14 m sq. (Llyn Hiraethlyn IV) to around 36 m sq. (Figure 11). They comprise turf ramparts, surviving up to 0.5 m high and 4 m wide in places, with external, now shallow,

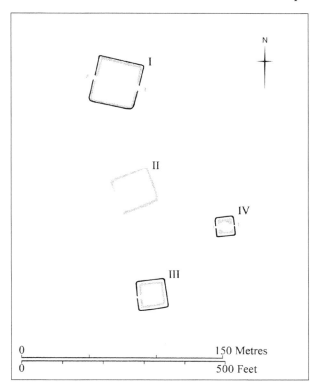

11. Plan of the four practice camps at Llyn Hiraethlyn in Merioneth.

slightly boggy, ditches. Entrances are recorded in some of the camps and two, camps I and IV, have two central entrance gaps protected by additional lengths of ditch (*tituli* – see Chapter 8). Their proximity to the Roman road, small size and clustering confirm their interpretation as practice camps. Indeed, there are over fifteen practice camps now recorded in the vicinity of the fort at Tomen-y-Mur[18]. Only Llandrindod Common, south of the Roman fort of Castell Collen in Radnorshire, has more in the vicinity, with some twenty-two small practice camps now recorded (see Chapter 6)[19].

CLASSIFICATION

Although the division between these four functions seems relatively clear-cut, in practice this is often not the case. Camps outside forts are frequently regarded as marching camps, although some could have housed troops involved in the fort's construction (with not all of them housed within the fort's perimeter, contrary to the ideas noted earlier). The wide range of sizes of camps along Hadrian's Wall means that it is difficult to categorise these in the same way as those along the Antonine Wall, although a handful have been tentatively proposed as probable practice camps[20].

To take a further example, outside the fortresses at Chester and York lie further groups of camps which are larger than those conventionally interpreted as practice camps using the criteria outlined above (ranging from around 0.5–1.8 ha and more). Some sixteen are now known running in an arc outside the Chester fortress[21], with four known outside York (out of a possible eight recorded in the eighteenth century)[22]. The practice camps recorded in Wales are largely located outside auxiliary forts, and it therefore seems likely that auxiliaries and new recruits were being trained in the craft of building camps. Those outside Chester and York, as well as being larger, might perhaps be associated with legionary field training and manoeuvres, representing camps that did house troops, even if these troops were on exercise rather than campaign. They are certainly very different in size from the conventional practice camps in Wales. On the continent, similar clusters of camps are recorded around legionary fortresses such as at Xanten (Vetera) and Bonn in Germany and Brigetio (Komáron) in Hungary, and are a similar size to those near Chester and York[23]. There can be little doubt that these camps were able to, and almost certainly did, accommodate soldiers in tents, although the purpose and length of their stay is unknown. Excavations in the interior of one of the camps outside York revealed little evidence apart from a few pits and post-holes of unknown date.

There was presumably an element of manoeuvres and military training in the construction of many camps, when physical defences were not necessarily demanded by the prevailing conditions. For example, in the first century AD, the Roman general Corbulo is recorded as establishing discipline among the troops through detailed and rigorous training regimes[24]. Those outside the legionary fortresses at York, Chester and on the continent may be considered evidence of troop movements in those areas and probably should not be grouped in the same category as the very small practice camps common in Wales, where practice is both identifiable through form and potential context, demonstrating evidence for concentration on elements of camp building rather than occupation, and therefore training in building camps rather than manoeuvres.

Elsewhere, clusters of camps are recorded outside various forts, particularly in the frontier zones of Britain (in the English–Welsh Marches and southern Scotland). These are not usually interpreted as camps for troops on manoeuvres but represent marching camps housing troops involved in campaigns and/or policing activities. In the Wroxeter area in Shropshire, the site of a fort, fortress, campaign base (at Leighton) and later Roman town (Viroconium), numerous marching camps have been found, suggesting that this area was a major springboard for operations west into Wales as well as north into Cheshire. They are located on the route of the Roman road which ran from south to north in this area, as well as on the River Severn running west into Wales. One of these, Cound Hall, is one of the largest known camps in this area, enclosing between 21 and 24 hectares (52–60 acres), and may have been a mustering base where differing forces combined prior to campaigns to the west (Figure 12)[25]. At Lochlands in Stirlingshire, next to the fort of Camelon, just north of the Antonine Wall where the Roman road from the south crosses through the Wall and heads further north, a cluster of over a dozen camps, frequently overlapping one another and therefore dating to differing periods, are now known. This site, representing a marshalling point for east–west communications along the line of the Wall as well as on the road north, was probably the main stopping point for all forces moving through the area (and some of the camps may have been involved in industrial activity relating to the occupation of the Wall – see Chapter 8).

The ephemeral nature of the archaeological remains and lack of systematic exploration of Roman camps mean that there are many questions to be asked with regard to their specific

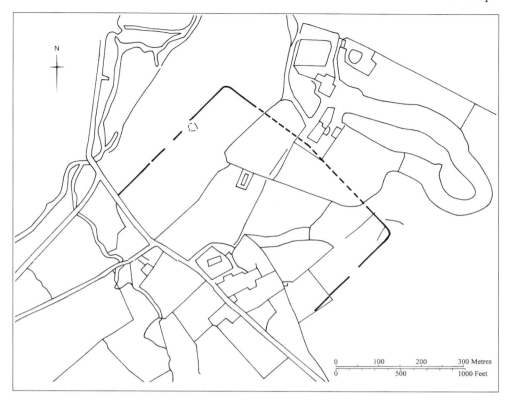

12. Plan of the camp at Cound Hall in Shropshire.

functions and dating. But a combination of archaeological analyses of the information gathered thus far, combined with literary and historical sources and comparative evidence, at least enable us to start to build a picture of what Roman camps were used for, as well as informing us about the daily life of the soldiers. Those camps which are, at present, 'lost' to the archaeological record by not being provided with physical remains which can be detected and interpreted are currently impossible to classify (see Chapter 8). For example, a temporary camp that later developed into a permanent fort could be difficult to detect without modern excavation, and even that might prove inconclusive. Furthermore, if a camp were not defended by the erection of a bank and/or the cutting of a ditch, then it too would be difficult to detect using modern methods of survey and interpretation. For example, the general Germanicus, a member of the Imperial family in the early first century AD, is reported to have pitched camp in Germany with earthworks to front and rear but palisades on his flanks[26]. Only the earthworks would be likely to leave an archaeological trace, although the recovery of palisades, particularly on later prehistoric sites, is well documented in the archaeological record. But the incidences of two parallel linear crop-markings are so frequent as to preclude their identification as Roman without excavation and further supporting evidence. There are undoubtedly many camps which await detection in Britain and beyond, and other functions for temporary structures out with the four outlined above.

4

Historical Sources

We are fortunate that a number of military treatises and historical sources with information about the activities of the Roman army have survived to be utilised and interpreted today. Many of these have previously been discussed in a book on the Roman Art of War[1], to which the reader is referred for more detailed information on the subject.

The exact origins of the Roman camp or fort are unclear, but it has been proposed that they were an innovation by the Greek King Pyrrhus of Epirus in the early part of the third century BC. This suggestion is based on the writings of Frontinus, Governor of Britain in AD 73/4–77, and the Roman historian Livy (writing in the early Roman Empire), although another account by the first to second-century AD biographer Plutarch claims that Pyrrhus himself observed the Roman field entrenchments, not the other way around[2]. One of the earliest depictions of an apparent temporary military camp appears on an Egyptian relief of the thirteenth century BC[3]. This relief, at the temple of Ramesses II at Abu Simbel, represents the clash between Egyptians and Hittites at the Hittite fortified city of Qadesh (or Kadesh, now Tell Nebi Mend in Syria), and depicts an Egyptian encampment surrounded by a square palisade of shields with two entrances. Ramesses' royal tent dominates the centre of the image, surrounded by soldiers undertaking preparations for the battle; the similarities between this and the later Roman military layout are remarkable and, according to the sources (the epic poem by Pentaur, the official Egyptian record), the camp was attacked, therefore demonstrating the need for its defended perimeter.

Further references to fortified encampments occur in classical literature, suggesting that the Greeks and Persians sometimes constructed entrenched enclosures while on campaign[4], reinforcing the idea that military camps were used by ancient armies before the Roman dominance of the Mediterranean world. To what extent the Roman army developed its own methods of fortification independently of other armies, or copied ideas from its enemies, is unknown, but it is clear that, in the latter part of the Roman Republic and during the Roman Empire, the art of castrametation (building camps) had evolved to leave the archaeological remains that can still be detected today.

There are similarities between the regimented design of Roman camps and contemporary Roman town planning, both possessing grid street patterns. The Roman surveying instrument known as a *groma* was used by both military and civilian surveyors when laying out space (Plate 6). One classical author, writing around AD 100, commented on the similarities in plan between camps and colonies, both having four gates and using a *groma* set up at the crossroads for surveying[5]. While there are some inaccuracies in this particular text (the author refers to a *forum* in the centre of the camp, whereas the *principia* or headquarters building would have occupied this location), it highlights the application of Roman surveying techniques to the planning and layout of both military and civilian settlements, and the apparent similarities between military and town planning. Certainly the regular ground plan of some of the Roman Republican colonies and, indeed, the Greek colonies, with their grid street pattern and external defences, echoes the layout of Roman military camps, and the similarities between military and civil planning. Indeed, Vegetius (see below) described the military camp as a 'walled city' which the Romans could carry around anywhere[6].

The first detailed study of Roman camps can be found in Polybius, a Greek writing in the second century BC. Polybius' History includes a digression on the Roman military system, including details on the layout of a military camp for a consular army of two legions, with comments on the layout for a double consular army of four legions[7]. Although his histories end in *c.*146 BC, it is from about this time that some of the Republican camps in Spain (in the area around Numantia) are believed to date[8]. Polybius' digression provides a valuable insight into the army of his day. His description of a Republican camp has enabled the creation of various schematic diagrams displaying the geometric morphology of a camp and the layout and disposition of troops within, and is frequently used in discussions of Roman camps in Britain despite representing the army of the Republican period rather than the Empire. In the mid-eighteenth century, General William Roy (see Chapter 6) included an entire section with illustrations on the Polybian camp in his study of the Romans in North Britain[9]. From Polybius' account, it appears that a simple formula for the camp was regularly adopted, although deviation from the regular square (or rectangular) form that he describes is evident in the archaeological remains of camps of the second century BC in Spain[10].

It is generally accepted that Polybius had witnessed the Roman army at first hand against the Greeks, and in writing his histories he utilised an additional earlier Roman source (or sources), possibly a Roman military handbook[11]. It seems quite likely that there were a plethora of military manuals created and used throughout the later Roman Republic and during the Empire, some of which are named in later sources[12].

Julius Frontinus, Governor of Britain in AD 73/4–77, wrote '*Art of War*' (*de scientia militari*, *de officio militari* or *de re militari*), possibly immediately after his return to Rome from Britain, which is now sadly lost. However, his subsequent *Stratagems* (*Strategemata*) has survived, comprising four books which quote examples of military stratagems. No single book in the *Stratagems* is dedicated to the construction of military encampments (presumably that was covered by his *Art of War*), although they are frequently mentioned in the military examples cited. It is interesting to observe that Frontinus is generally credited with the subjugation of much of modern-day Wales (particularly the Silures of southern Wales), with the completion of his campaigns against the Ordovices (in northern Wales) credited to his successor, the governor Agricola[13]. It is possible that Frontinus put some of his military training ideas into practice during and following the conquest of Wales, which could mean that the regimes of practice camps predominant in Wales started under his governorship (see Chapter 3)[14].

One of the prime historical military treatises for castrametation in the Roman Empire is a text on fortifying or surveying a camp, referred to as either *de munitionibus castrorum* or *de metatione castrorum*, credited to a writer often nicknamed 'Pseudo-Hyginus' (but referred to here as Hyginus)[15]. Much has been written about the potential date of this treatise, ranging from the first to the third century AD, although the favoured date is generally the second century AD, probably during the time of the Emperor Marcus Aurelius (AD 161–80) and potentially associated with his campaigns on the Danube[16]. However, the treatise may not have had such an obvious practical application and actually represent military theory, with the army detailed in the text purely hypothetical[17].

Although a fascinating military manual, Hyginus wrote about a large army which included detachments of the Praetorian Guard, thereby suggesting the presence of the emperor. Although such an army never took to the field in Britain during the period in which he was writing, in the early third century AD the Emperor Septimius Severus and his sons did undertake campaigning in northern Britain (see Chapter 5).

The last relevant military treatise is the *Epitoma Rei Militaris* by Vegetius, which is a general manual on military science written between AD 383 and AD 450, possibly for the Emperor Theodosius I (AD 379–395) and therefore probably in the latter part of the fourth century AD[18]. Despite this late date for the treatise, and Vegetius famously bemoaned the lack of knowledge of camp building by his day[19], it is clear that he used earlier sources which may be of more relevance to the period of conquests in Scotland. Certainly he cites Cato the Censor (the Elder), Cornelius Celsius, Frontinus and Paternus, as well as constitutions of Augustus, Trajan and Hadrian (the principles and precedents for the government of the Roman Empire), and he may have used a cut and paste approach to his sources with the addition of further information and interpretation[20], perhaps providing some insight into the earlier Roman sources, some of which were contemporary with campaigns in Britain.

Although Vegetius complains about the lack of camp building by his time, suggesting a lack of rigorous standards and lax practices, he may well have been exaggerating. He implies that the decline set in from the time of Gratian, emperor from AD 367–383, and his remarks may be intended partly as a sideswipe at Gratian or the House of Valentinian (AD 364–394) and need not necessarily represent the actual reality of the army in all the provinces. It need not have been the case that the army in Britain ceased to build camps, particularly in campaigns on the northern frontier against the Picts and Scots. However, despite literary evidence for late campaigns by the Roman army in Britain[21], hardly any archaeological evidence for campaigns in the fourth century AD has been recovered, and is currently limited to sherds of a Roman pottery beaker dated to the third to fourth century AD from a pit in Kintore in Aberdeenshire and occasional stray coin finds[22]. Dating evidence from camps in Britain is extremely rare, the majority of evidence suggesting occupation in the first and second centuries AD with occasional third-century stray finds.

Nevertheless, Vegetius provides us with a useful overview on the construction of camps[23], and agrees with Hyginus on various points, such as the rectangular shape of camps (whose length is one-third longer than the width). Ammianus Marcellinus, writing in the fourth century AD, mentions camps, reinforcing the suggestion that they had not completely fallen out of use as a military tool. Furthermore, a late sixth-century AD Byzantine treatise on military strategy attributed to Maurice refers to the building of camps[24]. No doubt the Byzantine army would have had access to the texts on Roman military strategy and been aware of the defensive methods employed in camp construction. By the later Byzantine period, the term *aplekton*[25] appears to have been used to indicate fortified camps, and this word is linked with a fiscal obligation on the local community to provide lodgings for troops that are passing through their territory.

Returning to the period of the later Roman Republic and Empire, one other useful contemporary source is *The General*[26] by the Greek philosopher Onasander, written in the first century AD and dedicated to Quintus Veranius, possibly the same Veranius who was governor of Britain in AD 57–8. It is very much a treatise on the characteristics and abilities of a general, but it does include comments on the fortification of camps.

Alongside the military treatises, a number of historians also furnish additional information on the construction and use of temporary camps. The works of the Greek historian Polybius have already been noted, and to this can be added the writings of the Jewish historian Josephus, who composed a tract on the Jewish War of the first century AD in which he included a digression on the Roman military routine[27]. Julius Caesar's accounts of his own conquests and battles in Gaul and the civil wars of the first century BC also furnish us with contemporary chronicles of Roman warfare, and frequently make passing references to camps from which further information can be gleaned, despite the personal propagandist nature of his writings. In particular they provide descriptions of the siege works constructed around the Gallic stronghold of Alesia in France[28]. The first-century BC Roman historian Sallust's account of the Jugurthine War in North Africa in the late second century BC also contains asides on the importance placed by the Roman Consul Metellus on camp construction and discipline[29]. Metellus' rigour for training and regulation are highlighted by other classical authors[30]. Furthermore, there are the surviving works of the key historians of the Republic and Empire, Titus Livius (Livy) writing in the late first century BC and early first century AD, Publius Cornelius Tacitus writing in the late first and early second centuries AD, the Greek Cassius Dio Cocceianus writing in the third century AD, and Ammianus Marcellinus writing in the fourth century AD. The writings of Tacitus, in particular, contain information about the Roman conquest of Britain, and in addition to his *Histories* and *Annals* he wrote a biography of his father-in-law, Agricola, governor of Britain from AD 77/8–84. This biography has been over-used to construct a geography of Agricola's campaigns, and thus interpret the available archaeological evidence, from the time of General William Roy in the eighteenth century to the present (see Chapters 5 and 6). There are, of course, numerous other historians from whom fragments of text survive, but it is these who provide the most valuable contemporary or near contemporary accounts and supply additional details on Rome's armies.

Finally, mention must be made of the Column of Trajan in the Imperial Forum in Rome (Plate 7), and the less famous Column of Marcus Aurelius. Both columns have friezes which depict campaigns on the Danube; that of Trajan relates the story of two Dacian Wars (AD 102–3 and AD 105–6) and that of Marcus Aurelius his wars against the Marcomanni (AD 172–3) and the Sarmatians (AD 174–5). Several friezes on Trajan's Column depict the Roman army building fortifications[31]. However, it is likely that the sculptors did not know

13. Detail of a relief showing a camp on Trajan's Column. © Angus Lamb, reproduced by kind permission of Professor David Breeze

the intricate details of Roman military life, and were depicting the army at work in the most suitable graphic way (Figure 13).

In contrast to the detail presented on Trajan's Column, that of Marcus Aurelius concentrates on the war itself rather than the methods employed by the army and is of less obvious use in studying the physical constructs of the Roman army in the field.

There is an apparent wealth of historical source material on the contemporary Roman army that has survived from antiquity, ranging from military handbooks through histories and biographies to sculptural relief. However, the relevance of these to the archaeological remains of the Roman army in Britain should not be taken as absolute. Tacitus' biography of his father-in-law, Agricola, has been used as an archaeological indicator for parts of Britain and has, as a result, had a tendency to skew interpretations of the evidence. Literary and sculptural sources should be seen in their historical context, secondary to the archaeology rather than as a primary dating mechanism. Nevertheless, they provide additional flesh on the bones of the archaeology and provide welcome additional information, even though this information must often be treated with caution.

5

Layout and Holding Capacity

LAYOUT

As observed in Chapter 4, historical sources provide a level of information about the internal layout of camps. For example, Polybius (writing in the second century BC), informs us that Republican camps were constructed by a simple ordered formula: the site was chosen, the area with the best view was selected for the *praetorium* (general's tent and headquarters) and measured out, the tribunes' tents were pitched in a line along the front of this with space for their baggage and mules; the camping ground for the legions, including the cavalry, was selected in front of the tribunes, the area to the side of these being allocated to the cavalry and infantry of the allies, with their infantry facing the camp perimeter. Behind the tribunes' tents lay the *forum* (market), the office of the *quaestor* (junior magistrate in charge of the legion's affairs), some *extraordinarii* (elite allies) and additional volunteers, again with the infantry facing the exterior of the camp. At the back of the camp were situated the remaining *extraordinarii* and other allied troops (*auxilia*). The German classical scholar Ernst Fabricius attempted a recreation of the layout of a Polybian camp (Figure 14)[1]. Following the completion of this internal layout of the camp, the rampart and ditch was constructed by both Roman and allied troops, supervised by the centurions and tribunes[2]. Attempts have been made to identify some of the camps in Spain with this layout, particularly around Numantia, but such claims must be treated with caution[3].

The disposition of a Republican camp described by Polybius differs slightly from the layout of camps of the Roman Empire[4], not least due to army reforms in the late second century BC and military reorganisation during and following the civil wars of the first century BC, particularly under the Emperor Augustus.

Polybius seems to make no space allocation for either camp followers (*lixae*), such as merchants and prostitutes, or slaves. Yet other (later) classical sources make it apparent that these were frequently inside the camp. For example, the Latin author Valerius Maximus, writing in the first century AD about events in the late second century BC, reported that, 'camp followers mingled with the soldiers and roamed about with them by day and night', only to be expelled by the Roman Consul Metellus upon his arrival[5]. Scipio Africanus the Younger expelled, 'traders, prostitutes, clairvoyants and diviners' on arrival at a camp close to Numantia during the Celtiberian Wars of the second century BC[6], reinforcing what is inferred from the Polybian camp layout that such followers were not permitted to camp within the Roman enclosure. Furthermore, in the mid-first century BC, Caesar reports that Cicero confined his troops to their camp, allowing not a single camp follower to pass beyond the entrenchment,

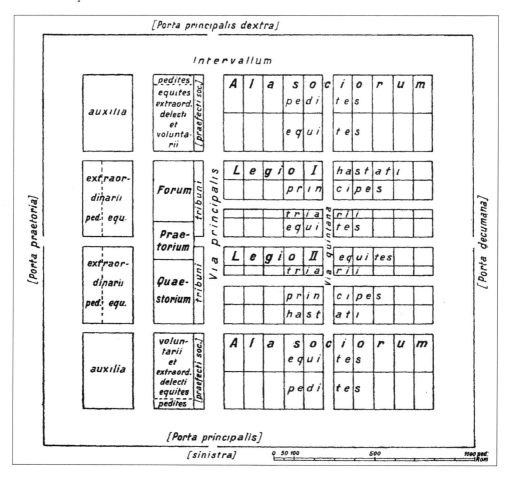

14. Schematic drawing of a marching-camp, based on Polybius' Histories, made by Ernst Fabricius in 1932. (Reproduced from the *Journal of Roman Studies* 1932)

implying that their inclusion within the camp was not out of the ordinary, although elsewhere he refers to traders camped outside but close to the rampart of the camp[7]. This perhaps suggests that they could enter and roam the camp but not actually stay there overnight.

Hyginus, who provides us with the most detailed information on the internal layout of the camp from classical sources, also makes no provision for camp followers. Given Metellus and Scipio's earlier actions, it is possible that their inclusion within the camp was seen as bad practice and therefore had no place in any military manuals. However, there is also no mention of space for slaves but these may have been included in the space allocation for troops without being specifically highlighted. Indeed, it is believed that slaves played a vital support role for the army but their likely numbers remains unknown. When referring to the baggage train, Vegetius does refer to servants occupying the centre of the column, together with the baggage, pack-horses and vehicles[8], but otherwise they are difficult to trace from the evidence currently available.

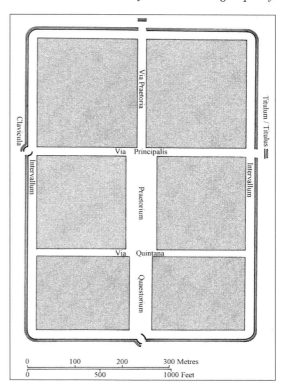

15. Schematic drawing of a marching-camp, based on Hyginus' *de munitionibus castrorum.*

Hyginus supplies detailed dimensions for the actual amount of space allocated to each component of the camp[9]. For example, a century of eighty men occupies a space of 120 Roman feet by 30 Roman feet and, although only eight tents are pitched (with eight men [a *contubernia*] occupying each tent and sixteen men on guard duty), the remaining space is taken by the centurion. This means that the space for a complete cohort (480 men) is 120 by 180 Roman feet, totalling 21,600 sq Roman feet. This equates to about 35.5 m by 53.2 m, an area of some 1,890 sq m (0.19 ha). The *praetorium* is described as measuring 720 Roman feet (213 m) long by 140–220 Roman feet (41–65m). The section of the camp in front of the *praetorium* is known as the *praetentura*, that to the side, the *latera praetorii*, and the area behind as the *retentura* (Figure 15).

Hyginus also describes the various roads in the camp: the *via principalis* runs in front of the *praetorium* to the two side gates of the camp, the *porta principalis dextra* (right) and the *porta principalis sinistra* (left), and should be 60 Roman feet (17.7 m) wide, the same width as the *intervallum* road running between the camp perimeter and the troops. Another road, known as the *via sagularis*, runs around the camp, between the legionary cohorts encamped around the edge of the camp and the troops quartered further within. The *quaestorium* (office of the *quaestor*) is located in the *retentura*, and is where any hostages or booty will be placed. The road behind the *praetorium*, parallel to the *via principalis*, is known as the *via quintana*. The rear gate is known as the *porta decumana*. Hyginus gives details of where each section of the army that he describes should camp, including cavalry (*ala*) and auxiliary troops. A sufficient amount of information regarding this particular army (of *c.* 40,000 troops) is presented to enable detailed reconstructions to be made of the internal arrangement of troops of the army described[10].

This level of detail in internal layout is not equalled in any of the other surviving texts. Vegetius supplies information on the measurements of the ditch and rampart, but very limited specifics on the internal arrangements, merely commenting that the area enclosed should correspond to the size of the army[11]. While this seems an obvious and logical statement, several classical texts give examples of troops being crammed into a small camp, or leaving a small portion of the army in a larger camp with instructions to light fires to make it appear to the enemy that the entire camp was still occupied[12].

The ancient authors also consider where camps should be sited; the Greek philosopher Onasander, writing in the first century AD, noted that a good governor should 'choose a locality that is not marshy, nor damp; for such places by their rising vapours and rank smell bring disease and infection to the army, and both impair the health of many and kill many, so that the soldiers are left few in number and weakened in strength'[13]. This agrees with the more detailed texts supplied by Vegetius and Hyginus on the need to change camp frequently to avoid disease, and the importance of choosing a good site close to a spring to provide a good source of water for the camp's occupants[14]. Furthermore, a later Byzantine source also argues that the force should move regularly, every few nights, for reasons of health. Indeed, Hyginus provides a detailed account of where camps should be situated:

> Concerning the choice of terrain for the establishment of the camp; first they chose a site which rises gently above the plain, on a distinctive rise and the *porta decumana* is set at the highest point so that the area is dominated by the camp. The *porta praetoria* should always look towards the enemy. The second place is situated on a flat plain, the third is on a hill, the fourth on a mountain, the fifth in whatever place is necessary, from which it is called an unavoidable camp ... Unfavourable positions were called mothers-in-law [lit. 'stepmothers']][15]

The military manuals, by necessity, portrayed an idealised view of the location and layout of a military camp. In practice, the army seems to have been more pragmatic, although hints of a 'jobsworth' mentality can be detected at times. The camp at Arosfa Garreg in Carmarthenshire encloses a steep ravine down to a stream in its south-west quadrant, which would have provided awkward camping ground for the troops despite potentially providing an internal water source[16]. This camp is of standard rectangular shape and perhaps indicates a preference by those laying out the camp to adherence to military standards. This can be contrasted with the camp at Plumpton Head in Cumbria, where the surveyors took care to avoid an area of boggy ground, creating an irregular perimeter in the process (see Chapter 9)[17].

The camp at Hindwell Farm in Radnorshire, on the border with Herefordshire and Worcester, is an example of a camp sitting on a low ridge (in the Walton Basin) with good views in all directions (Plate 8). Four other camps and a Roman fort are also recorded in the immediate vicinity (see below and Chapter 7). Although the location of the *porta decumana* is unknown, the camp appears to possibly face south-east towards the nearby Roman fort,

16. Aerial view of Twyn-y-briddallt in
Glamorgan, taken from the north-west
in 1999. © Crown Copyright: Royal
Commission on the Ancient and Historical
Monuments of Wales. 995103-45.

which would place the rear of the camp on slightly higher ground[18]. It is interesting to note
that most of the camps in Wales had the *porta decumana* sited at the highest point on the
circuit[19], confirming Hyginus' suggestion that the camp then dominates the area.

In contrast to Hindwell Farm, the camp of Twyn-y-briddallt in upland Glamorgan sits
on the end of a ridge between two river valleys (Figure 16). Although the area surrounding
the camp has been relatively recently re-forested, its topographical position (at about 440 m
above sea level) suggests that it would have had commanding views in most directions[20]
(on the assumption that much of the surrounding landscape had been cleared of woodland
by the time of the Roman occupation). Although the camp is not rectangular, it conforms
to the shape of the ridge, demonstrating that those involved in laying out the camp felt
that utilising the topography for military advantage was more important than following a
rigorous manual requiring camps to be specific shapes.

Another dictat stated by Hyginus was that the surveyors should avoid siting the camp
close to woodland and, indeed, Caesar refers to an occasion when German horsemen
were able to attack the camp, having been screened by a nearby wood[21]. However, the
environmental evidence for large parts of Britain suggests that it had been largely cleared
of trees in the Bronze and Iron Ages, and the avoidance of woodland would have been
potentially less of an issue for the Roman army campaigning in Britain. Indeed, this may
not have always made it easy to find 'sufficient supplies of firewood'[22].

Hyginus' text refers to several legions encamped together[23] and no doubt camping
the Roman legionaries and auxiliaries (allied soldiers) together represented an economy

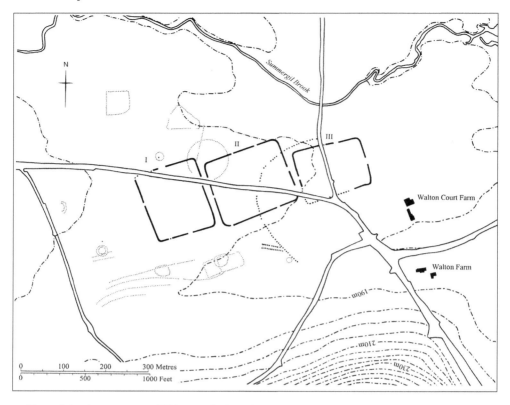

17. Plan of the three camps at Walton in Radnorshire.

of effort when it came to constructing the perimeter defences as well as encouraging camaraderie and competition among the army on campaign. That this was standard practice is exemplified by some of the extremely large camps recorded in northern Britain, which must have held several legions and auxiliaries. However, legions did not always encamp together, for example, Josephus refers to Titus' armies constructing three separate camps for differing forces on their arrival outside Jerusalem, prior to the siege[24].

Returning to the Walton Basin in Radnorshire, close to Hindwell Farm, three camps lie on a very similar alignment, separated by less than 15 m (Figure 17; also see Chapter 7). Although no dating evidence has been recovered, it is possible that the occupation of the three was chronologically close, with the consecutive arrival of three units of similar size creating a concentration in this area, or it could represent forces arriving too soon after the previous occupation to wish to use the 'soiled' area occupied by the preceding force[25]. These camps can justifiably be considered a British mirror to Titus' three at Jerusalem. A similar situation of three camps, although not in such regular alignment, is noticeable at Farnley in Northumberland, a short way south of Hadrian's Wall[26].

Polybius, Vegetius and Josephus all refer to surveyors laying out the internal area of a camp first, followed by the perimeter. Although Tacitus highlighted that Agricola chose the sites for pitching camp himself[27], in practice it was more likely that the camp prefect (*praefectus castrorum*) performed this role, and that Tacitus was just emphasising what a good general Agricola was. Josephus informs us that three trumpet calls sound the order to break camp: on the first call the tents are dismantled, on the second they are loaded onto the baggage train and on the third the marching column sets out. We are also informed as to the order of march, with surveyors and engineers marching in the vanguard and therefore arriving at the next camp site early enough to lay out the necessary space requirements prior to the arrival of the main force, who would be engaged in the camp's construction. The importance of setting out the internal space first is also implied by Hyginus, who concentrated on the internal layout before discussing the perimeter defences. The duty of the choice and location of the camp was allocated to the camp prefect (*praefectus castrorum*), a senior army officer who also had responsibility for the soldiers' tents and baggage. He had the choice of the location of the camp, ensuring that it was a suitable size to enclose the army. The marching column of a large force could be extremely long, covering many miles, with the head of the column potentially arriving at the next camp site shortly after the tail of the column had left its predecessor. A fourth-century AD account of the AD 363 Persian expedition of the Emperor Julian (AD 355–63) refers to the marching column extending over ten miles at one point[28].

An army marching from camp to camp would presumably have required exactly the same space from one to the next and the troops could therefore have started the building of the perimeter rampart and ditch once they had arrived before the interior layout was constructed – it would presumably have been very quick and easy to allocate the internal space required and begin the demarcation of the perimeter. However, this is on the assumption that the area to be enclosed was fairly regular and special circumstances (such as topographical considerations, as with Twyn-y-briddallt earlier) would not have required a shift in the alignment of part of the defences. The archaeological remains of camps in Britain demonstrate that no two camps are identical, although on occasions camps do have very close dimensions. For example, the camps of Cornhill II in Lanarkshire and Strageath Cottage in Perthshire have almost identical dimensions (470 m by 290 m, enclosing 13.8 hectares (34 acres), Figure 18) but are geographically dispersed, being located over 83 km from one another. Cornhill II represents a reduction in size of an earlier, larger camp, and possesses additional ditches (*tituli* – see Chapter 8) at two of its gates. The form of protection utilised at the entrances of Strageath Cottage is unknown.

Elsewhere, particularly north of the Forth-Clyde isthmus, groups of camps do have similar but not identical dimensions, and can be grouped into particular 'series' suggesting the march of troops on specific campaigns (see Chapter 9). Camps that can be grouped in this way usually enclose very similar overall areas and share morphological characteristics (such as the number and type of gates and conformity of shape). The same camp prefects were presumably deployed and the camps enclosed the same army so we would expect conformity between successive camps built and utilised by the same forces.

It is therefore clear from the classical sources that they supply valuable information regarding the internal layout of the camp and the area required to house armies of different size and composition. These at least enable hypothetical reconstructions of marching/campaign camps to be created, and an assessment of the number of troops that each camp was able to hold. However, they also suggest many different reasons for the nature of the archaeological

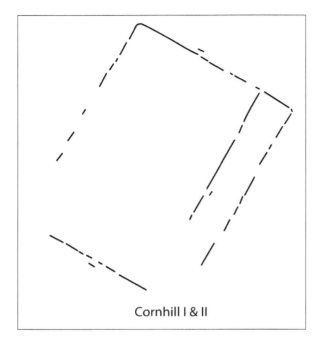

Cornhill I & II

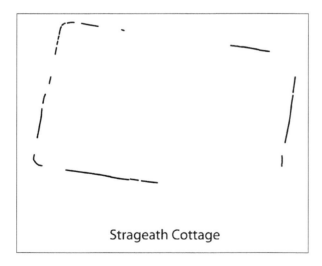

Strageath Cottage

18. Drawing of the camps of
Cornhill II and Strageath Cottage.

remains that survive today, from large numbers of troops brigaded together in larger camps to separate legions building camps in close proximity to one another. Furthermore, this concentration in the surviving classical texts on marching or campaign camps appears to leave us in a literary wilderness with regard to the other camp functions identified in Chapter 3. This is not entirely correct, because there are numerous narrative sources for sieges across the Roman Empire, although few tell us much about the form a layout of Roman siege camps[29]. Classical sources tell us little about housing troops undertaking construction activities, and only slightly more with regard to practice camps, although Vegetius informs us that a recruit should learn how to build camps[30], and the writers Appian and Tacitus tell us about the training regimes demanded by the generals Scipio Africanus and Corbulo[31].

ORIENTATION

When it comes to the orientation of camps, Vegetius states that they should face east, or towards the enemy, or the line of march[32]. It is not known why Vegetius states that a camp should face in an easterly direction, unless it has to do with the rising sun. It has been suggested that it may have been a Christian influence[33], but the Persian king Cyrus in the sixth century BC also made it his custom to have his tent pitched facing east[34]. Furthermore, we are also told that the rear portion of the camp (*retentura*) should be at its highest point[35]. Siting the rear rampart of the camp on a crest would avoid dead ground on that side. It was earlier observed that during fieldwork in Wales, a large number of the camps could be seen to have had their rear gate, the *porta decumana*, sited at the highest point on the circuit, indicating the importance of local topography when laying out a camp.

Inside a camp, the headquarters or general's tent (*praetorium*) faced towards the front of the camp with one road leading out through the *porta praetoria* with the cross roads in front of the *praetorium* (the *via principalis*) leading to the side gates (Figure 14). Due to the forward position of the *praetorium*, these side gates were often located closer to the front of the camp than the rear.

When it comes to the archaeological evidence from Britain, it is clear that the achievement of all the ideals stated in the texts of Hyginus and Vegetius with regard to camp location and orientation was rare. This is particularly true in some of the larger camps, where availability of enough suitable ground would have taken preference over concerns of orientation. Indeed, it is clear from the topographic location of most camps in Britain that the primary concern for the camp builders was to identify a piece of ground suitable for camping.

Although the potential forward location of the side gates should enable us to determine the direction in which a camp faced, a combination of factors including lack of clarity in identifying entrance positions, questions over direction when six gates are present, and the sufficient survival and/or visibility of enough of the camp perimeters mean that it is difficult to state with confidence the orientation of many of the camps in Britain. We can be reasonably confident of the orientation of around 20 per cent of these, and there are two options for around 50 per cent, usually due to uncertainty over the position of the side gates (or because the camps have two gates in their longer sides – six in total). However, in the case of the latter, other factors such as topography and direction of march may help to assess the camp direction, although determining this assumes that we know the route and objective of the travelling army. It is presumed that many marching camps represent the halting points for invasion forces into territory (enabling speculation over the direction of march), but other interpretations can be made for many of these.

The instruction that the camp should face the enemy probably relates more to camping in advance of pitched battle than to an army operating generally in Britain, where it appears evident from the classical texts that pitched battles were infrequent and it seems from what we know of warfare in the north and west that there was no obvious 'front' and that the enemy might be expected to come from any direction. However, the camps for which orientation is considered known include a number along the line of the Antonine Wall. These camps, broadly lying to the south of the Wall, all face in a northerly direction (including north-east and north-west), unsurprisingly towards the line of the Wall.

Elsewhere, a number of camps face a nearby fort, demonstrating that this was the focus and thereby indicating a chronological relationship between the two (but not necessarily implying that the camp was a labour or construction camp for the fort). The fort of Castledykes in Lanarkshire, for example, sits among a number of marching camps which have been re-used several times (evidenced by additional ditches within camps, reducing the space for the entrenched forces) (Figure 19). The majority of these camps appear to face the general direction of the fort (except camp IV on Figure 19, the orientation of which we do not know, and the unknown southern side of this camp may have a relationship with the fort annexes). On the Roman road of Dere Street, running from York into Scotland (towards Edinburgh), quite a number of camps appear to directly face the road, possibly suggesting that they post-date its construction, whereas others appear to face the general direction of march northwards up the route of the road, but the relationship between these camps and the road is uncertain. Although only an either/or direction can be ascertained for some of the camps along Dere Street, it is worth considering this further. Many camps are sited on a level terrace or ground which gently undulates, but occasionally there is a noticeable slope. On these occasions, a further handful of camps can be assigned an orientation if the surveyor adhered to the classical dictum of placing the *porta decumana* on higher ground; of these, exactly half face in a general easterly direction.

Thus we cannot state with any certainty that the camps in Britain attempted to face in an easterly direction, despite Vegetius' dictum. But it is also worth observing that Hyginus says nothing about facing a particular compass direction, instead proposing that the camp should always face the enemy[36].

Unsurprisingly, if all camps faced the enemy, then the enemy was located in all directions, because there is little obvious symmetry. This is perhaps to be expected when an army is newly campaigning in possibly hostile territory beyond the existing conquered part of the province. However, there is a tendency for the camps along Dere Street to either face the road or the route of the road northwards, and quite a number of the camps in Dumfriesshire face in a westerly direction, presumably the general route of march across south-west Scotland. When orientation can be determined along some of the river valleys, it appears that many

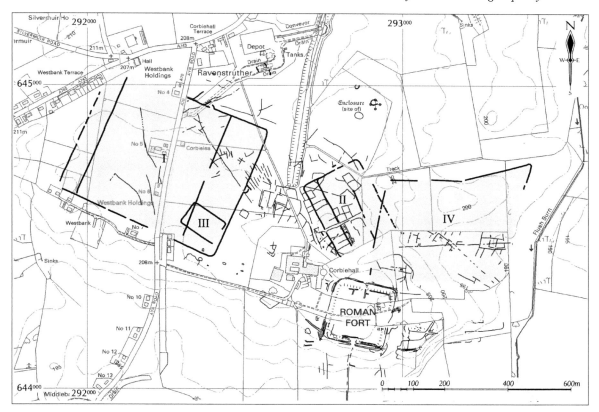

19. Plan of the camps at Castledykes in Lanarkshire.

of the camps face the river, but this is perhaps only to be expected when access to fresh water supplies would have been extremely important, and when a road is present as well, many face the road rather than the river. At the very large camps found in northern Britain, it is clear that the prime concern of the camp builders was to orientate the camp to suit the topography: terrain was the prime motivator of orientation. It surely must have been the case that the allocation of a sufficient amount of usable space to house troops and conduct the other necessary activities of the camp was paramount, alongside access to suitable water supplies. All this would have been far more important than direction of orientation, and illustrates the fragility of the link between military manuals and practical necessity.

HOLDING CAPACITY

It is apparent from the literary sources that the size of the camp ought to reflect the number and type of troops quartered within its perimeter. Topographic considerations play a role when calculating the number of troops that can be quartered, although it is clear from the archaeological field evidence that the camp surveyors attempted to locate as much as possible of the camp on usable ground[37].

The information that Hyginus provides is valuable but any exercise to adapt his methodology to camps in Britain is purely theoretical. Nevertheless, various attempts have been made by scholars over the years to assess the holding capacity of marching camps, usually expressed in terms of the number of men per acre or hectare, although no formula has gained universal acceptance. There are numerous variables at play here: we cannot know the composition of a transient army in Britain without detailed historical and/or epigraphic information, although inscriptions found in forts sometimes tell us the name of the garrison that was housed there for a period of time, and artefacts can provide other clues to the ethnicity of soldiers stationed in a particular area[38]. Centurial stones on Hadrian's Wall, stones that give the names of centurions (or occasionally other soldiers), and distance slabs on the Antonine Wall (see Chapter 3) tell us the units that constructed sectors of these frontiers. Furthermore, ink writing-tablets from the Roman fort of Vindolanda, discovered since the 1970s, furnish further details of specific units on Hadrian's Wall[39]. Other evidence such as bronze military diplomas, issued to soldiers on their discharge from the army (or in other exceptional circumstances) and granting Roman citizenship, supply information as to the auxiliary units stationed in particular provinces at certain points in time[40]. However, no historical detail is available to inform us of the exact composition of a campaigning army, and the exact garrison of Britain at any point in time can only be estimated.

Even Tacitus' biography of his father-in-law gives only limited information regarding the exact make up of his army. For example, at the battle of Mons Graupius, Tacitus informs us that Agricola had 8,000 auxiliary infantry in the centre with 3,000 cavalry on the flanks; the legionaries and a further four *alae* (of around 2,000 cavalry) were stationed in reserve[41]. Therefore, there appear to have been some 13,000 auxiliary (allied) troops, and a large Roman legionary force composed of an unknown number of soldiers, probably taken from all four legions stationed in Britain at that point (the *II Adiutrix*, *II Augusta*, *IX Hispana* and *XX Valeria Victrix*). In theory, the legions numbered a total force of some 20,000 men, but in reality some detachments would have remained at the legionary headquarters, some had been posted to the continent, and it is possible that one or more legions may have been under strength[42]. Speculation about troop numbers has led to proposals that Agricola's army at the battle would have numbered somewhere between 20,000 and 30,000 men[43], although figures at the lower end of this scale are usually preferred, and perhaps between 17,000 and 21,000[44]. Even with the detail that Tacitus provides us for Agricola's troops in this battle, it is still not possible to agree on the size of his army and therefore the way that this might possibly translate to the size of a temporary camp hosting that force. In addition, without knowledge of the exact location of the battle and therefore the identification of likely camps that housed Agricola's forces, assessments of space allocation and camp sizes remain speculative exercises.

Looking to the military manuals, those of Polybius and Hyginus have been used by various scholars to suggest calculations of density of men within temporary camps, frequently using various archaeological sites as case studies (see below). General William Roy, who did have first-hand experience of troops under canvas, also made an attempt at this in the eighteenth century[45]. He used Polybius to suggest that a legion on its own could be accommodated in an area of 338 yards by 336½ yards (309 m by 307.7 m), thereby some 23.5 acres or 9.5 ha. On the basis that a legion during the time of Polybius would have numbered some 4,200 men[46], this equates to some 178 men per acre, or 442 men per hectare. If the legion were larger, perhaps numbering closer to an Imperial legion, then this figure could increase to in excess of 200 men per acre. Since then, numerous other attempts have been made to reconstruct Hyginan camps and work out troop densities of varying proportions[47]. Some of the higher-density interpretations may suggest a camp that was overly cramped, and certainly could imply that some of the extremely large camps found in Scotland housed enormous armies. But there is, by necessity, a crudity in these figures, because any assessment needs to take account of the varying size of the *praetorium*, the width of all internal streets, the width of the *intervallum*, and any space that may be allocated for slaves, mules and other *impedimenta* (baggage).

Turning to the archaeology, attempts have been made at various camps to assess their holding capacity. The camp at Rey Cross, astride the A66 in County Durham, is almost a parallelogram in form and encloses some 8.1 ha (20 acres) within nine known gates, and possibly had eleven if the Roman road from York to Carlisle entered and exited the camp at a further two gates, as seems likely from their spatial positioning[48]. General Roy initially assessed that the camp at Rey Cross was the work of a single legion (he postulated the *legio VI Victrix*)[49]. Taking the figures crudely, this would calculate its holding capacity at around 250 men per acre (630 per hectare) if this represented a legion at full strength, an only slightly higher density than that which he calculated from Polybius (see above). The presence of so many gates at this camp allows theoretical street lines to be drawn on the ground plan of the camp, enabling a potential subdivision. This exercise was undertaken by Richmond and McIntyre and, on the basis of this castrametation (the making or layout out of a camp), they divided the internal area into twelve similar-sized blocks of ground and two larger areas (Figure 20)[50]. From this they proposed that the camp housed a single legion (some 5,000 men) with a single auxiliary detachment occupying the same space as a cohort, and therefore possibly a quingenary cohort (of around 480 men). Undertaking the same exercise as that proposed for Roy, this calculates to a density of around 280 men per acre (690 men per hectare), although elsewhere 300 men per acre (740 per hectare) was advocated[51]. It has also been proposed that the same force occupied the nearby camp at Crackenthorpe in Cumbria, which has similar morphology but is slightly larger at 9.3 ha (23 acres; also see Chapter 9). However, not all the internal space of this camp would have been suitable for pitching tents due to the presence of a deep internal gully, and a subsequent reduction would result in a similar useable space to that at Rey Cross. This variability between the sizes of these two camps, which are often grouped together, demonstrates a problem when attempting to fit armies into a basic camp area without considering topographic and other elements of their field archaeology that might affect the useable space within the camp.

A similar exercise in castrametation has been applied utilising Hyginus' methodology to suggest an alternative garrison[52]. This proposed that the camp could hold a legion plus a complement of auxiliaries which would amount to one milliary *ala* (a cavalry unit nominally some 720 strong), one milliary part-mounted cohort (infantry and cavalry of around 1,000), one quingenary part-mounted cohort (infantry and cavalry around 600 strong), two quingenary infantry cohorts (around 480 men each) and some scouts, totalling

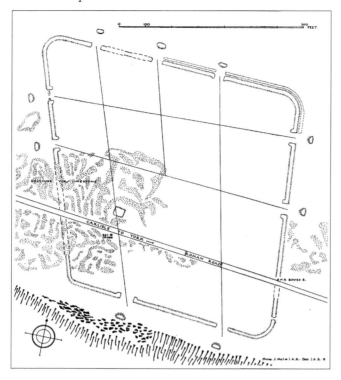

20. Plan of the proposed layout of the camp at Rey Cross in County Durham, from Richmond and McIntyre in 1933. (Reproduced from the *Transactions of the Cumberland and Westmorland Antiquarian and Archaeological Society*, 1934)

8,640 men. This therefore implies a density of some 460 men per acre (1,150 men per hectare), a much higher level of crowding than that proposed by Roy and Richmond and McIntyre.

A further exercise has been conducted on the camp at Inchtuthil in Perthshire, on the basis of lines of pits that have been revealed through aerial photography[53] (Figure 21). These pits are assumed to have been disposal pits running along the sides of rows of tents potentially demarcating street lines. Although the exercise was purely speculative and deals with a partial crop-mark record, it has been estimated that Inchtuthil II (a camp of some 18 ha/44 acres) might have held a mixed legionary and auxiliary force (of infantry with a complement of cavalry) totalling 12,500 men. Gordon Maxwell calculated a density of 284 men per acre (694 men per hectare). Adjusting the size of the camp slightly through re-appraisal of the air photographs to 19.8 ha/49 acres, this figure reduces to some 255 men per acre (628 men per hectare), and is similar to Roy's estimations for Rey Cross. Another study, working closer to Hyginus' methodology, proposed a force of 21,825 men, giving a density of 445 men per acre (1,097 men per hectare)[54]. However, this may have been too large an army and perhaps a force closer to 25–27 cohorts, or even fewer, would be more likely. Twenty-seven cohorts, if of regular rather than double strength, suggests that some 12,960 men occupied the camp. Despite the much higher figure given through an analysis of Hyginus, this lower figure is far closer to that proposed by Maxwell. However, whatever the density of Inchtuthil II (and indeed its reduced form, Inchtuthil III), it may not represent the norm because, if it housed troops engaged in the construction of the neighbouring

21. Aerial view of the camps at Inchtuthil in Perthshire. © Crown Copyright: RCAHMS. SC359708. Licensor www.rcahms.gov.uk

legionary fortress, then their differing function and lengthy occupation might suggest a different density to that of marching camps.

Abroad, exercises in troop disposition have been undertaken at siege camps such as the Republican camps at Numantia in Spain and also at Masada in Israel. But their differing function and potential longer occupation than marching camps means that the troop density may well have been different. The camp at Renieblas, near Numantia, contained stone-built barracks which, it has been argued, reflect the tented field layout described by Polybius[55]. At Masada, the remains are also so well preserved in stone, with internal compartments visible, that attempts have been made to assign unit strength to individual siege camps surrounding the Jewish stronghold. It is generally proposed that two of the Masada camps (B and F) housed a complete legion (the *legio X Fretensis*) split between the two, and that the other camps housed auxiliary units (Figure 1)[56]. If the legion were at full strength then this represents a crowded interior by comparison to the figures proposed elsewhere, all the more surprising when the troops knew that they were to be stationed there for a period of time and the prevailing extreme temperatures in desert conditions. The density could be up to 584 men per acre (1,444 per hectare), and 426 men per acre (1,053 per hectare), but there are discrepancies between the plans of the Roman remains by various scholars. If the legion were under full strength, the density figures could reduce to 291 men per acre (720 per hectare). This is closer to the figures cited by other scholars at other camps, but again sounds a health warning about the dangers inherent in allocating camp density figures when the actual details of the occupying garrison are unknown. Assessments in general at Masada seem to suggest a density range from 307–404 men per acre (760–1,000 per hectare). Furthermore, this assumes that similar spaces to stone buildings were also allocated to troops under canvas, without making allowance for differing needs and conditions.

Other attempts at calculations of camp density have concentrated on the use by the Roman army of the *actus* when laying out the camp. The *actus* is a unit of length measuring 120 Roman feet and is derived from the term for 'driveway' from agricultural practices. Two square *actus* joined together is referred to as a *iugerum*, which therefore represented an area of 120 by 240 Roman feet. The *actus* was used by Roman land surveyors when dividing up the landscape (centuriation)[57].

It has been suggested that many camps were laid out utilising the square *actus*. Maxwell used the small camps of around 1 hectare in size round Chester and York to suggest that a quingenary legionary cohort of 480 men would have required 8 sq. *actus* (which equals 1 hectare), each century requiring about 1 sq. *actus* with additional space for the rampart and *intervallum*[58]. This gives a density of over 620 men per hectare (240+ men per acre) or 480 per hectare (194 per acre) if strictly using the one cohort per hectare method. Further arguments for the use of the *actus* by the Roman army have been made, including the suggestion that a cohort required 2 sq. *actus* ('*actus quadrati*') and that cavalry troops had four times the space allocation of infantry[59]. This equates to around 480 men per acre (1,186 per hectare), a high density similar to that proposed by some of the analyses of Hyginus noted earlier.

While the densities proposed by these two methodologies differ considerably, the use of the *actus* by the Roman army has much to commend it. The grouping of a number of camps at around 2 hectares in size suggests 16 square *actus*, potentially two cohorts according to the lower density calculations, or between five and eight using the higher density figures. But eight cohorts in a 2 ha (5 acre) camp seems very high and potentially cramped, and would indicate a gigantic army if scaled up to some of the larger camps found in Britain. Many of the camps on the Antonine Wall are around 2 ha in size (see Chapter 3) and if the troops quartered in these camps were engaged in construction duties on the Antonine Wall, the reality might well lie in the lower figures, which could reflect a more accurate estimation of the likely numbers of men available to be deployed[60].

The camp at Logie Durno in Aberdeenshire is frequently cited with regard to its holding capacity due to being one of the favoured locations for the Roman army quartered for the battle of Mons Graupius against the Caledonian tribes[61] and being the largest camp in northern Scotland, enclosing almost 57 hectares (144 acres) (Figure 22). Some debate has

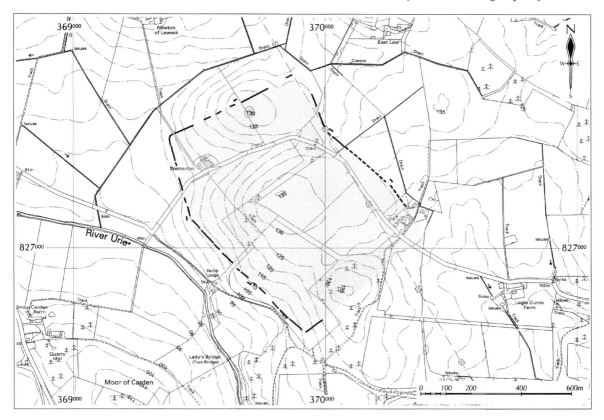

22. Plan of Logie Durno in Aberdeenshire.

focussed on the holding capacity for the camp, and the possibility that it was too large to host the size of the army that fought with Agricola (discussed earlier). Using the various methodologies cited above, the army numbers range from 28,100 men to over 70,000 men. Even utilising the figures from Masada again produces a high occupancy count of 61,000 men. Yet the men may not have been closely crowded together and space would have been laid out for other activities. In addition, Tacitus informs us that Agricola's forces marched light in that season and presumably, therefore, had less baggage[62].

Indeed, none of these exercises fully take account of the space that would have been required for the baggage animals who usually accompanied the army on campaign and, also, sufficient space for the horses for cavalry units. That is because these are not quantified in sufficient detail in the available sources and difficult to detect archaeologically. Assessments of the possible make up of the forces campaigning in Britain, whether the army that invaded Britain in AD 43 or the troops accompanying Agricola at Mons Graupius, have proposed that a large number of baggage mules were used and they would have required space within these camps as well as plentiful supplies of food and water[63], although, as noted earlier, Agricola may have travelled with fewer baggage animals in his final season.

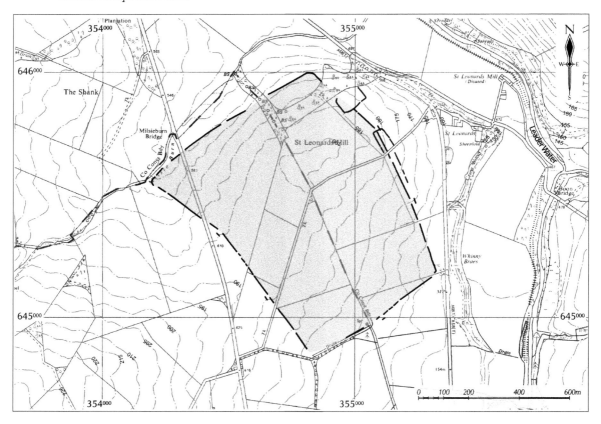

23. Plan of St Leonards in the Scottish Borders.

The largest camp known in Britain, and one of the largest in the Roman Empire, is that at St Leonards in the Scottish Borders (Figure 23). This camp encloses some 70 ha (173 acres), and is sometimes associated with the campaigns of Septimius Severus in the early third century AD on the basis of its huge size and the assumption that the force campaigning with the emperor in northern Britain was the largest ever seen and therefore occupied the largest camps (see Chapter 9). Applying the same formulae to St Leonards as noted above for Logie Durno, the holding capacity of the camp ranges from 40,000 to 85,000 men, but it is interesting to note that application of calculations made by William Roy in the eighteenth century come to the lower end of this spectrum, and he had directly comparable experience of troops under canvas[64].

Even allowing for a large area of space allocated to the emperor and the presence of the Praetorian Guard, high density figures must be surely too cramped for an army in the field. At the time of Severus' conquest, only three legions were stationed in Britain (as opposed to four during Agricola's campaigns in the first century, though he had lost detachments to Germany), but with the probable addition of the *legio II Parthica* and the Praetorian Guard, Severus may have had the equivalent of six legions (*c*. 30,000 men) on campaign with him[65]. Assuming that he also had a large complement of auxiliaries, then this figure could almost double, but not every soldier in Britain would have been on campaign with the emperor, and many of the existing forts and fortresses will have maintained a standing garrison. The historical sources inform us that Severus mustered additional resources to form a powerful army and that he lost as many as 50,000 men during the campaign. Although this figure must be an exaggeration, it does indicate the vast size of the army deployed[66]. Certainly, the presence of the emperor, with all the support staff that he needed to run the Roman Empire from a hillside in the Scottish Borders and the, no doubt huge, baggage train, would have necessitated an extremely large area be given over to the temporary stations of the army. Severus was also reported to have come to Britain with a high sum of money, which would no doubt have required additional space, staff and security[67]. Using the most generous figures for space allowance within the camp and the presence of a large baggage train, St Leonards could have held at least 40,000 men, surely the largest army that ever took to the field in Britain, excepting perhaps the Claudian invasion army[68].

The two largest camps in Britain that have revealed evidence for occupation in the first century AD are the camps at Carey in Perthshire (Figure 24) and Kintore in Aberdeenshire (see Chapter 8). Both enclosed over 44 hectares (110 acres), the former revealing a single sherd of late first-century AD samian pottery during limited excavation of the ditch, the latter a suite of radiocarbon dates and finds suggesting a foundation in the later part of the first century AD (Flavian period).

The potential size of the first-century AD army operating in northern Britain with Agricola has already been noted and it is therefore possible that these camps can provide further clues to the possible holding capacity of camps, and narrow down the wide range noted earlier. Again, applying the figures from earlier, the camps could each hold between 21,000 and 52,000 men. It is interesting to note that the lower end of the scale, 21,000 men, is estimated to be around the likely size of force that Agricola had at his disposal in his final campaign.

Therefore, with the assumption that the size of the army which Tacitus describes as being available for the battle of Mons Graupius was not significantly larger during other first-century AD campaigns, the knowledge that Carey and Kintore were probably Flavian foundations can provide clues to the numbers of men that these large Flavian camps could have held. Certainly it seems highly unlikely that any more than 30,000 men were campaigning in north Britain in this period, and if, for example, Agricola had an approximately equal force of legionary and auxiliary troops, this suggests some 26,000 men in the field. Thus it seems likely that camp density was in the lower range of the figures that have been proposed above, and that the extremely high figures proposed through readings of Hyginus must be treated with caution, and the hypothetical nature of his work observed. The actual number of men stationed within the perimeter of the camps cited here must therefore lie somewhere between the extremes given, and almost certainly are at the lower end of the spectrum if the assessments relating to the number of men available to occupy Carey and Kintore are correct. Even if the tents were pitched relatively close together, there would have been space for wagons, mules, and other activity in the camp. Estimations have been made regarding the number of mules that would have been required for an army on campaign[69], and archaeology can furnish a little additional evidence. For example, excavations at the battlefield site of Kalkriese in Germany, where Germanic tribes destroyed

24. Aerial view of the camp at Carey in Perthshire, taken from the south in 1978. © Crown Copyright: RCAHMS. SC1234191. Licensor www.rcahms.gov.uk

three legions under their commander Varus in AD 9, have so far revealed finds relating to animal harnessing as well as the skeletal remains of eight horses and thirty mules, no doubt a fraction of that which accompanied the army on campaign[70]. However, the amount of space given over within camps to baggage and mules remains an unknown variable.

It is worth commenting that, despite far greater evidence of the internal arrangements within forts and considerably more extensive excavation over several decades, the density and composition of fort garrisons is also often unknown. Although several attempts have been made to correlate fort types with particular garrisons, there is still disagreement and any direct correlation between internal fort area and the size of the garrison difficult to sustain. For example, at the later first-century AD (Flavian) fort at Elginhaugh in Midlothian, despite significant area excavation revealing eleven barracks, of which at least six were interpreted as stable barracks, it was not possible to be fully confident about the nature of the occupying garrison[71]. While excavations on fort barracks have led to the identification of stabling areas, no such level of confidence is currently possible within the interior of temporary camps, and the ratio of cavalry to infantry for a campaigning army remains an unknown quantity which can only be estimated. Although some of the historical sources can indicate the make up of specific armies at particular points in time, such as the troops at Agricola's disposal in his final season and at the battle of Mons Graupius, noted earlier, even these do not give us precise figures because not all the legions and auxiliary units may have been at full strength, and the number of mules required remains an unknown factor.

Despite the various valiant attempts that have been made to assess the numbers of troops quartered within a camp, they are subject to numerous variables: topography, the ratio of legionaries to auxiliary troops, the ratio of infantry to cavalry, the number of mules and size of baggage train, the possible availability of space for camp followers, the space allocated to the *principia*, and the potential presence of the emperor and his large household in some circumstances. Furthermore, evidence from the bronze military diplomas and Vindolanda writing tablets indicate that detachments of troops were regularly stationed elsewhere. Furthermore, evidence from Dura-Europos on the Euphrates (in modern-day Syria) suggests that units may have been under strength at various points in time[72] and we cannot always assume the standard figures for legionary and auxiliary regiments.

That there were standard ways of laying out a camp are clear from the surviving texts and the broad similarity visible in the form of surviving camps, enabling groupings on the basis of size and morphology to be made. That this standard method was centred on the use of the *actus* is persuasive, and certainly some form of calculation based on the Roman foot must have been used. It is interesting to note that the argument that approximately one *actus* was given to each century would produce an army of approximately the size suggested by historical sources for the camps at Carey and Kintore[73]. The argument for the use of the *actus* is also supported by the excavations at the Roman fort of Bearsden on the Antonine Wall in East Dunbartonshire; much of the internal layout of the fort is now known and the excavator has suggested it was laid out using the *actus*[74].

When it comes to the surviving texts, Polybius was writing about a different army and period to the conquests in Britain. Hyginus, while providing some of the detailed mathematics, does not give sufficient information, and his figures must therefore be considered with the caveats noted earlier. Seeking to determine the number of troops quartered within a camp is important when trying to assign potential chronologies to camps on the basis of the knowledge that we have from other sources on the size of the army in Britain at certain points in time. Large-scale excavations in camp interiors, as at Kintore in Aberdeenshire (see Chapter 8), may furnish additional clues to holding density. But until further excavations have taken place, providing more information, we remain wedded to the existing sources noted earlier, and some variability in the calculations on camp occupation will remain. Such paper exercises as have taken place on the number of troops quartered within a camp are useful in determining perhaps the minimum and maximum number of troops that a camp could hold, but until more is known about the variables noted earlier, these remain hypothetical. When excavators of permanent forts with plans of barrack blocks cannot be sure of the numbers of men and the nature of the unit that was housed within, our confidence level in the application of statistics and formulae to the holding capacity of temporary camps must be tempered. Nevertheless, despite the hypothetical nature of the assessments of camp density, it does seem likely that the lower end of the scale, perhaps somewhere between 480–690 men per hectare (200–275 men per acre) is closer to the actuality of the Roman army that operated in the field. Even using the lower figures, we are still presented with the notion of huge armies occupying the larger camps in northern Britain, even if a considerable amount of space was given over to other activities than housing for troops. Finally, our knowledge of the size of the Iron Age population of Britain during the Roman period is limited and we have to accept an element of bias and exaggeration when figures for warbands are provided by the classical texts. For example, Tacitus tells us that Agricola faced a force of more than 30,000 Britons at the battle of Mons Graupius, of whom some 10,000 were killed. However, considering that Tacitus also created an entire speech for their leader, Calgacus, one has to question the accuracy of this account, which may well have seen the figures massaged in Agricola's favour[75].

In conclusion, it must be accepted that assessments of troop numbers obtained by applying classical texts to archaeology remain highly speculative. Even the extensive excavations of pits and ovens at Kintore in Aberdeenshire (see Chapter 8) have not clarified the picture with regard to the number of men stationed within. But this exercise in calculating troop numbers has been performed since the time of General William Roy in the eighteenth century (see Chapter 6) and no doubt will continue to be an area of interest for the foreseeable future.

6

History of Archaeological Discovery

ANTIQUARIAN TRADITION

Britain is extremely fortunate to have had a strong tradition of antiquarian interest in the Roman period. Major Roman monuments such as Hadrian's Wall have long been a subject for study[1] but interest in some of the less substantial structures grew from the eighteenth century. Antiquarian monographs such as Camden's *Britannia*, first published in Latin in 1586 with English translations from the early seventeenth century, demonstrate a growing interest in Roman structures. Identification of temporary camps was generally undertaken by men of landed backgrounds, for whom antiquarian pursuits were a wealthy man's hobby and many of whom collected artefacts as well as compiling journals of their visits and contributing to various studies. Military men and the clergy were the other two principal groups who identified Roman camps. The former were interested in the campaigns of earlier armies, particularly those with an accompanying literary tradition. Even Edward I, King of England, is said to have carried a copy of Vegetius' *Epitoma Rei Militaris*, a present from his wife, during his campaigns in Wales in the thirteenth century. Men of the clergy would have been familiar with a number of classical writings including those of Josephus, who wrote about the Jewish War (see Chapter 4), which would have given them knowledge of the campaigns of the Roman army.

The practice camps on Llandrindod Common, south of the fort of Castell Collen in Radnorshire, Wales, were identified by the Reverend Thomas Price in 1811, described as 'a young but intelligent and zealous antiquary' by Theophilus Jones in a letter to the editor of *Archaeologia*[2]. Price recognised their Roman character and was concerned that they might be destroyed due to the enclosure of the commons and their cutting for fuel. He recorded and planned eighteen, and speculated as to their function, but struggled with their precise function due to their number and proximity to one another (Figure 25). His account was picked up by Jonathan Williams, writing a *History of Radnorshire* in 1856, who suggested that the camps were thrown up by the invading army, one after another, in an attempt to gain ground from the Silures.

It was not until 1936, and probably as a result of discussions with the German scholar Ernst Fabricius over the function of some of the temporary camps at Haltwhistle Burn in Northumberland, that the Durham University academic Eric Birley suggested that they were the product of the Roman army's field-training activities[3].

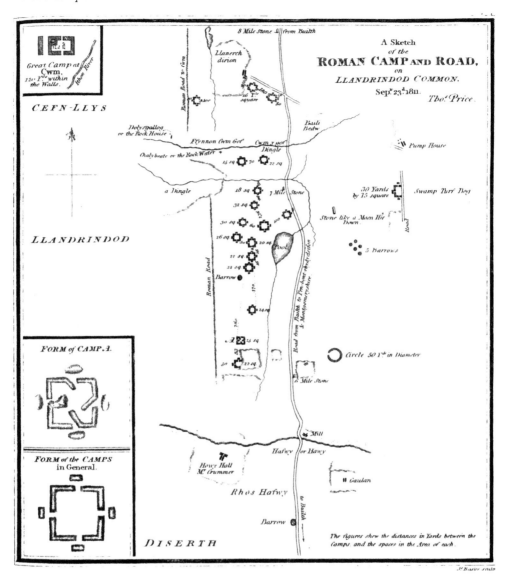

25. Plan of the camps on Llandrindod Common, made by Reverend Thomas Price in 1811. (Reproduced from *Archaeologia* 1814)

The remains of fourteen of the eighteen camps recorded by Price were surveyed in the 1960s, with the remainder having been destroyed by the construction of the spa town of Llandrindod Wells; some twenty-one or twenty-two are now believed to have been recorded, either as low earthworks on the ground, or as crop-markings on aerial photographs[4].

In the mid-eighteenth century, Captain (later General) Robert Melville was keen to reconstruct a geography of Tacitus' *Agricola* in northern Britain. He was convinced that the battle of Mons Graupius between Agricola and Calgacus must have happened towards the

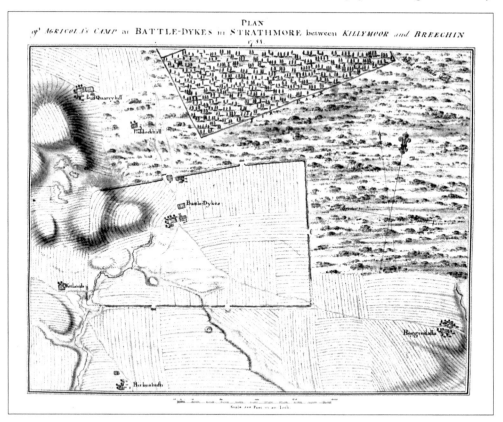

26. Plan of the camp of Battledykes Oathlaw in Angus, made by William Roy in 1755. (Plate XIII from 'Military Antiquities of the Romans in Britain'). © Courtesy of RCAHMS (Society of Antiquaries of London). SC923908. Licensor www.rcahms.gov.uk

eastern extremity of the Grampian Mountains, and in 1754 he travelled through Strathmore, discovering four new camps, no doubt guided by local place names such as Battledykes and Wardykes[5]. Melville was in communication with a number of contemporary authors[6] and also conveyed his enthusiasm to William Roy, a young assistant on the Military Survey of Scotland[7], and explained to him the difference between temporary camps and more permanent stations. Roy planned Melville's new discoveries in 1755 and went on to make the greatest contribution to Roman camp studies before the twentieth century. Roy's detailed plans of Roman structures in northern Britain were published in his magnum opus on the *Romans in North Britain*, produced by the Society of Antiquaries of London in 1793, three years after his death[8].

Roy's approach to surveying methods was pioneering at the time: he was awarded the Royal Society's Copley Medal for Science in 1785, following the measurement of a baseline on Hounslow Heath, and paved the way for modern cartography and surveying, and the start of the triangulation of Great Britain. The Ordnance Survey, of which he is regarded as one of the founding fathers, was established one year after his death. He produced by far the best plans of camps for over a century, and many of his measurements can be verified today.

27. Aerial view of the north-west corner of the camp of Battledykes Oathlaw in Angus and stretches of the adjacent sides, taken from the north in 1990. © Crown Copyright: RCAHMS. SC1164090. Licensor www.rcahms.gov.uk

The camp at Battledykes, Oathlaw in Angus was one of the camps discovered by Captain Robert Melville while travelling through Strathmore in August 1754 and planned by Roy the following year (Figure 26). When Roy planned it, most of the four sides were visible, along with five entrances, four of which were protected by additional stretches of ditch (*tituli*). A later eighteenth-century account by the Reverend Jameson of Forfar also records this as an enclosure, describing two ramparts with a ditch in between, presumably reflecting the survival of an upcast mound outside the ditch created by excavated material from the ditch[9]. By the mid-twentieth century, only part of one side survived, together with an external stretch of rampart and ditch (a *titulus*) protecting the entrance[10], but all that now survives is this entrance *titulus* close to the edge of a plantation, although much of the remainder of the camp has been recorded as crop-markings on air photographs[11] (Figure 27).

28. Aerial view of the camps at Swine Hill (Four Laws) in Northumberland, taken from the west in 1978. Photograph by Professor Norman McCord. © Newcastle University, ref. A078638/6

Later surveyors and field archaeologists to have had a significant impact on Roman camp studies include Henry MacLauchlan, a former member of the Royal Corps of Military Surveyors and Draftsmen, followed by employment with the Ordnance Survey and, in the mid-eighteenth century, commissioned by the Duke of Northumberland (a keen antiquarian) to carry out surveys of Roman roads in Durham and Northumberland and complete a magisterial survey of Hadrian's Wall[12].

In 1850–1, during a survey of 'Watling Street' (Dere Street) from the River Tees to the border with Scotland, MacLauchlan recorded numerous sites, including a new camp at Four Laws (also called Swine Hill), a few kilometres south of the Roman fort at Risingham in Northumberland (Figure 28). At this location, he recorded the earthwork of a camp with three gates visible, each with 'an inflexion of the rampart for its defence'[13] – his description of internal curved ramparts or *claviculae* (see Chapter 8); he recorded it as enclosing 6 acres. More recent field survey has confirmed the accuracy of his measurements[14]. As was the practice of his time, he attributed the camp to Agricola; although no date has been confirmed, a first-century AD date for the camp does seem more likely given the presence of *claviculae* at the entrances (see Chapters 8 and 9). A few years later MacLauchlan was busy with the survey of Hadrian's Wall and he included quite a number of the camps alongside the Wall in his survey, including Glenwhelt Leazes, where he captured the detail of the entrance gates, which possess both internal *claviculae* and external *tituli* (see Chapter 8)[15].

AERIAL SURVEY

Aerial survey and photography revolutionised our understanding of archaeology, particularly in the plough-levelled lowlands, in the twentieth century. Differential crop growth over the buried remains of ditches and walls is best viewed from an aerial perspective, where the viewer can trace archaeological features in the patterns formed on the ground. The buried ditches of temporary camps provide sources of moisture for crops in dry summer months and those crops lying above such features grow taller than their neighbours and change colour differentially from the rest of the crop. Temporary camps also have characteristic features, such as rounded corners and distinctive gateways (see Chapter 8), that enable them to be identified in the aerial record from other crop-markings (Figure 29).

The two world wars of the twentieth century significantly developed the technology of airborne reconnaissance, and one of the pioneers of air survey and photography in archaeology was Osbert Guy Stanhope Crawford, a member of the Royal Flying Corps during the First World War. In 1920, Crawford was appointed as the first archaeological officer of the Ordnance Survey and it was thanks to his dedication and knowledge that modern Ordnance Survey maps remain a rich source of information about archaeological sites. Although interested in a wide range of archaeology, Crawford had a particular interest in Roman archaeology[16] and this has been of huge benefit to Roman camp studies.

On a seminal flight into Scotland in June 1939, Crawford discovered a camp at Gallaberry in Dumfriesshire (Figure 30). The purpose of this flight was to investigate Roman roads and sites, partly in order to produce a third edition of the Ordnance Survey's *Map of Roman Britain* (eventually published in 1956). The camp is small in size, enclosing less than 0.7 ha (under 2 acres), and only a single entrance gap is known. It overlies a probable Neolithic cursus monument (a large elongated enclosure or ceremonial way) and is close to a small prehistoric fort.

Crawford's successor in the promotion of aerial reconnaissance in archaeology was (John) Kenneth Sinclair St Joseph, a member of the Royal Air Force (RAF) during

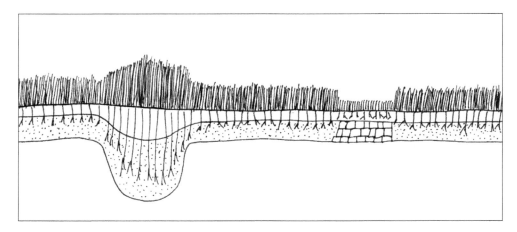

29. Schematic examples of differential crop growth, creating crop-markings which can be seen from the air.

30. Aerial view of the camp at Gallaberry in Dumfriesshire, taken from the east by O. G. S. Crawford in 1939. © Courtesy of English Heritage / RCAHMS. SC1164037. Licensor www.rcahms.gov.uk

the Second World War, but employed by Cambridge University from 1948[17]. St Joseph's research interests also lay in the field of Roman military archaeology and he was a key figure in expanding our knowledge of the Romans in Britain through his aerial discoveries. Although based in Cambridge, St Joseph frequently mounted long-range aerial campaigns into the north and west of Britain, stationing himself, pilot and aircraft away from home, and regularly published summary papers of his results in various journals. In particular, he wrote numerous synopses of recent aerial discoveries in Roman Britain for the *Journal of Roman Studies*. Thanks to this regular reconnaissance by St Joseph, our knowledge of the campaigns of the Roman army in Britain grew exponentially, especially in the lowland areas in the English–Welsh Marches and in the lowland areas of Scotland.

The camp at Auchinhove in Moray, one of the most northerly camps in Britain, was first recorded from the air by St Joseph in 1949, lying in a series of arable fields just to the south of the A95 from Banff to Keith (Figure 31). This camp, which possesses distinctive 'Stracathro-type' gateways (see Chapter 8), was subjected to small, exploratory trenching on

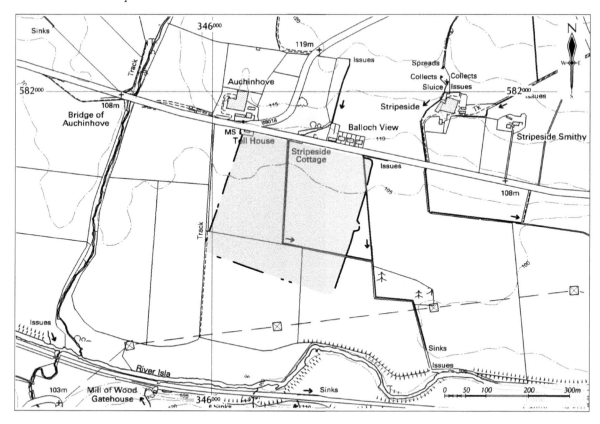

31. Plan of Auchinhove in Moray.

several occasions by St Joseph and colleagues. These confirmed his identification of the site as Roman and clarified which of two linear crop-markings on the south-west side of the camp represented the line of the camp[18]. St Joseph regularly 'ground truthed' his aerial discoveries and, although the recovery of dating evidence from such small-scale interventions is rare, small, targeted excavation campaigns like these enable us be confident of the precise forms of crop-mark archaeology that we can identify as Roman in date (also Chapter 8).

In tandem with the Cambridge flying programme, vertical air photograph collections (particularly the National Surveys taken by the RAF after the war) began to be scrutinised by archaeologists compiling various inventories across Britain. For example, archaeologists at the Royal Commission on the Ancient and Historical Monuments of Wales (RCAHMW), working on the Inventory of Glamorgan in the 1960s and 1970s, found three new earthwork marching camps through scrutiny of the air photographs[19]. In 1949, archaeologists at the Royal Commission on the Ancient and Historical Monuments of Scotland (RCAHMS) discovered a new Roman fort and camp at Oakwood while undertaking research work for an inventory of Selkirkshire[20] (Figure 32).

In numerous cases, it has been an interdisciplinary approach that has led to the discovery or rediscovery of many Roman camp sites. For example, a very large camp at Househill,

32. Vertical air
photograph of the camp
at Oakwood, taken by
the Royal Air Force
in 1946, and identified
by Feachem during
the preparation of the
Inventory of Selkirkshire
(RCAHMS 1957). The
four sides of the camp
are indicated, and
the additional arrow
towards the bottom of
the image marks the
Roman fort. © Crown
Copyright: RCAHMS
RAF Collection: 106G/
UK/0086 4437

Dunipace, in Stirlingshire was identified as indeterminate earthworks over a number of years from 1954 onwards, and it was only when these pieces of the jigsaw were fitted together with various air photographs in 1988 that the site's identification as a Roman camp was recognised. Another example was pieced together from the eighteenth-century antiquarian sources of the historian William Maitland, who had recorded a camp at Catermillie near Dundee which was only re-identified (at Invergowrie) through modern aerial survey in 1990. Both of these puzzles were completed by Gordon Maxwell, another archaeologist with strong Roman research interests, who established a Scottish-based aerial survey programme with the RCAHMS in 1976[21].

Finally, another example of a camp which was partially lost before being revealed again from the air is that at Grassy Walls in Perthshire, first planned by William Roy in 1771[22]. By the 1850s, the Ordnance Survey, engaged in surveying the County series maps, were able to record only the site location on the first edition map because the surrounding landscape had changed dramatically and the farm of Grassy Wells had vanished. It was recorded on the ground in 1917[23] but a new plan of the site was not produced until 1949 by Crawford, who claimed 'to have put it on the map'[24]. Some remains of the camp are visible today as earthworks but the majority is known from crop-markings on air photographs (Figure 33).

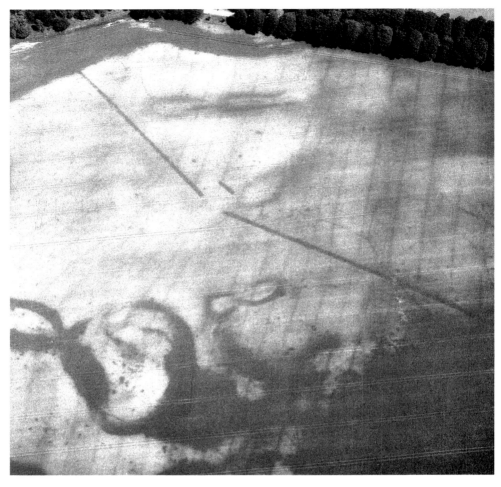

33. Aerial view of part of the camp (east side and entrance) of Grassy Walls in Perthshire, taken from the south-west in 1989. © Crown Copyright: RCAHMS. SC777927. Licensor www.rcahms.gov.uk

REMOTE SENSING

More recently, other forms of remote sensing have been applied to Roman sites with some interesting results. The application of airborne Light Detection And Ranging (LiDAR) is still in its early stages, but can help with the interpretation of slight earthwork remains and those under certain types of woodland. LiDAR uses an optical laser to produce three-dimensional data points at very close intervals, creating detailed topographic surveys. It has revealed occasional new pieces of evidence about existing sites, such as additional information about some of the sites on Hadrian's Wall. Indeed, a new camp has recently been identified using LiDAR close to the fort of Carrawburgh on the Wall (Plate 9).

Geophysical survey, such as resistivity and magnetometry survey, and ground penetrating radar, has been applied to Roman sites with excellent results. These involve the location

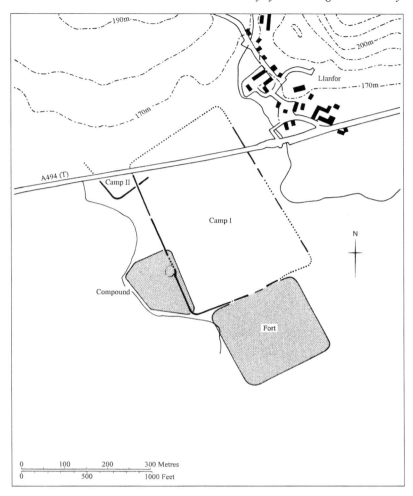

34. Plan of Llanfor in Merioneth.

of sub-surface features through measuring the resistance levels when electrical currents through the ground, or detecting magnetic differences in the soil, or using radar pulses, respectively. Two of the most successful recent campaigns of geophysical survey have been those around Roman fort sites in Wales and along Hadrian's Wall[25]. Indeed, geophysical survey has enabled more of the perimeters of some camps to be identified, revealed additional features such as possible ovens, and even identified new camps. At Dalswinton Bankfoot in Dumfriesshire, recent survey revealed possible ovens inside the camp (see Chapter 8) and at Hindwell Farm in Radnorshire, a new camp was revealed. At Llanfor in Merioneth, magnetometry survey of an existing site of a Roman fort, compound and temporary camp, all known as crop-markings through aerial survey, revealed a second camp, which overlapped the first, and it is curious that this camp has not been visible from the air (Figure 34). It is likely that in pastoral areas and those unresponsive to differential crop-mark formation, geophysical survey will play a major role in identifying and providing new information about Roman camps.

7

Re-Use and Survival

RE-USE

The number of camps across Britain still visible as upstanding earthworks demonstrates that many must have been left as extant features in the landscape by the Roman forces and were not slighted on departure. This is also evidenced in the way that many sites were re-used by the Roman army on more than one occasion (re-using either the general location or part or all of the perimeter of an earlier camp). The first-century AD Jewish writer Josephus informed us that the Romans 'fire the camp, which they can easily reconstruct if required, lest it might some day be useful to the enemy'[1], but this must not have been standard practice in Britain and, indeed, elsewhere in the Roman Empire where upstanding earthwork camps are recorded[2]. Excavations on the fort at Bearsden on the Antonine Wall in East Dunbartonshire recorded an area of burning outside the east rampart which the excavator interpreted as the timber breastwork from the rampart, thrown and burnt when the fort was abandoned, but there was no attempt to backfill the ditches and the remaining earthworks survived to be recorded in the eighteenth century[3].

Occasionally, excavations of camp ditches reveal turves from the ramparts in the fill of the ditch, but these may have been the result of natural slippage rather than the deliberate forcing of the rampart into the ditch. The remarkable state of preservation of camps in some places argues against attempts to deliberately destroy the remains. Not only would the existence of a camp in the landscape have been a reminder of the might and power of the Romans to the local population, but it also could be re-used by later forces. Or, indeed, usefully re-used by the local population themselves as a convenient enclosure for activities such as arable agriculture or animal husbandry. For the Roman military, returning to a camp site and re-using part or all of the perimeter of a previous camp could represent an economy of effort, assuming that the ground occupied by the camp was not too foul from its previous occupation (see Chapter 4), at which time the decision might have been taken to build a new camp next to the previous one rather than re-use the same area of churned up ground. This might explain some instances of camps being constructed alongside one another rather than re-using perimeters. There are numerous examples across Britain of pairs or more of camps located next to one another but establishing chronological relationships or sequences between these is difficult (also see Chapter 9).

In the Walton Basin in Radnorshire, close to the modern border with Herefordshire, some five marching camps surround the fort of Hindwell Farm. Three lie on a very similar alignment (see Chapter 4, figure 17) and are rectangular, enclosing between two and just over three hectares (5–8 acres). Despite their apparent uniformity, all three may face in slightly different directions, and one camp has evidence suggesting it may have been re-used at some point. That these three correlate with Josephus' descriptions of Titus' forces arriving in Jerusalem has already been noted (Chapter 4)[4]; trying to identify either sequence or date for them is extremely difficult, but Josephus' description suggests that they could possibly be contemporary with one another. We do not need to see these as belonging to different campaigns in Wales, or to successive units arriving so soon after the departure of a preceding force that they did not want to use ground that may have still been soiled or otherwise unusable.

Although it can be difficult to establish if camps alongside one another were constructed at different times or were contemporary, on numerous occasions overlaps can be seen between their perimeters (and sequences determined through field survey and/or excavation), or a later camp could utilise part of the perimeter of an earlier predecessor. But the troops quartered within the smaller camp would need to ensure that they could not be trapped in the open ground between the earthwork perimeter of their larger predecessor and the safety of the occupied camp. When there is a smaller camp inside a larger which re-uses some of the same sides, it is usually assumed that the smaller will be the later of the two, but on occasion this may not have been the case and each site would have to be taken on its own merits given the vast range of sizes of camps. These sizes are dependent on the scale of troop movements and the numbers of troops requiring to be housed, and if a larger force was in operation than that which previously occupied the camp, then it seems likely that a new camp would be built from scratch, and there are numerous examples across Britain where camps intersect one another without re-using part of their perimeters (for example, see Ardoch, Chapter 9). At Tomen-y-Mur East in Merioneth, the earthwork remains suggest that the smaller, inner camp might be the earlier, its remains being slighter than camp II, which appears to overlie it on one side[5]. At Birdhope in Northumberland, the smallest camp of the three known (none of which appear to share sides but lie within one another) appears to have had its rampart and ditch slighted, which may suggest that it was earlier in date than at least one of the two camps within which it lies[6]. Given what the classical authors have told us about the layout and location of the camp (Chapter 5), it does seem unlikely that a later camp would entirely enclose an earlier without significantly slighting any remains that blocked easy passage along the streets and around the *principia*.

However, a large number of camps where part of the perimeter is re-used are known only through crop-markings and, therefore, excavation would be required to ascertain the relationships between the structures. The best example of Roman camp re-use still surviving as an earthwork today is at Pennymuir in the Scottish Borders, close to the modern border with England, which are among the best-preserved camps anywhere in Britain. Lying in rough moorland in the Cheviot Hills, beside the Roman road of Dere Street, at least three and possibly four camps are now known. Two in particular are in an excellent state of preservation, with ramparts surviving over 1 m high and over 4 m wide, accompanied by similarly wide ditches whose earthwork remains are over 1 m deep in places and presumably would be revealed to be deeper if excavated. Entrance gaps protected by additional stretches

35. Aerial view of the camps I & II at Pennymuir in the Scottish Borders, taken from the south-south-west in 1995. © Crown Copyright: RCAHMS. SC505325. Licensor www.rcahms.gov.uk

of rampart and ditch (*tituli*) are clearly visible (Figure 35). Not only were the remains not destroyed by the Romans on departure, but the site was also reused. The larger camp encloses some 18 hectares (44 acres) with a second (enclosing less than 4 ha – under 10 acres) tucked into its south-east corner, utilising parts of the adjacent two sides. Indeed, this secondary camp may also have been re-used because one of its gates had been narrowed at a later stage[7].

The propensity for the Roman army to re-use existing locations, including the same camp sites, is clear when one looks at the numerous occasions when camps have been re-used, as at Pennymuir, sit beside one another, as at Walton, or overlap in their use of space. Close to the summit of Trecastle Mountain in the Brecon Beacons (Brecknockshire) lies the most extreme example of camps with overlapping perimeters, at Y Pigwn (Figure 36). Here, two camps survive as upstanding earthworks with ramparts and ditches clearly traceable on the

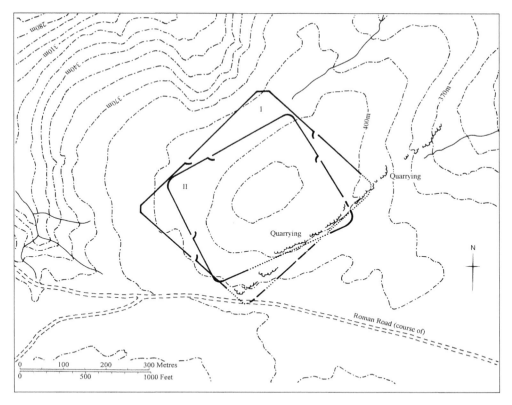

36. Plan of the camps at Y Pigwn in Brecknockshire.

ground. The smaller of the two is fitted into the earlier, larger camp at an oblique angle with only a slight overlap at the perimeter[8]. That there must have been time delays between the occupation of the two is apparent by the re-use of the same ground, and it is curious that the later camp was constructed at a different angle rather than re-use part of the perimeter of its predecessor. Perhaps this site hints at the mentality of those soldiers involved in establishing and laying out Roman camps, and also that the economy of effort through re-use of earlier ramparts and ditches was not felt necessary on this occasion.

Elsewhere, excavations of camp ditches have occasionally revealed evidence for their re-cuts, which had not been suspected through the existing earthwork or crop-markings, potentially indicating that the entire perimeter was re-used. Excavations at Dunning in Perthshire suggested that two of the entrances had been re-cut, although there was faint evidence for a secondary phase from the known crop-markings of the camp on air photographs which may not have been seen by the excavators[9]. At Dalginross, also in Perthshire, trenching on a gate recorded that it had been re-cut, but the crop-markings are so clear (see Chapter 8, Plate 14) that any additional ditches should be visible, again suggesting that perhaps the entire perimeter was re-used[10]. However, our knowledge of re-use of entire perimeters is slight, relying as it does on the excavated evidence of re-cut ditches. At Kintore in Aberdeenshire (see Chapters 8 and 9), it is the excavated finds assemblage that suggests more than one phase of occupation, but excavation of substantial areas of ditch produced no trace of a re-cut. The upstanding remains of some camps are still so good that one wonders to what extent a re-cutting of the ditch and/or refurbishment of the rampart would be required if the defences were left in prime condition and the timescale between re-occupations relatively short. Perhaps only minor rampart repair and ditch cleaning would be required, in which case any re-occupation could be almost invisible archaeologically. Alternatively, if a re-cutting of a ditch created one that were larger than its predecessor, then the re-cut could remove all traces of its precursor.

LATER SURVIVAL

After the departure of the Romans from Britain, the survival of these camp sites clearly depends on a number of factors: whether they were deliberately slighted, either by the Romans or others, whether the land on which they were sited was improved, re-used in some other form, built over, or otherwise changed in the intervening centuries. It is in the unimproved upland areas of Britain where the remains of camps are most visible, particularly in parts of Wales, in Northumberland, and in parts of Scotland. Even sites that were visible to antiquarians three centuries ago may now have had their surface traces obliterated, usually due to agricultural practices.

On occasions where the remains are not particularly well preserved, later landscape features might reflect the position of the camp's ramparts and ditches – elements that were once prominent earthworks. Frequently camp ditches have been re-used as field drains, and ramparts utilised as field boundaries. Occasionally, sections of camp perimeters survive thanks to woodland plantations, resulting in stretches avoiding the ravages of the plough. Sometimes, sections of camp ditches have been re-used within woodlands as forestry drainage ditches, but the remains are usually significantly damaged by such use and the ramparts destroyed. Elsewhere, earthen banks enclosing plantations might have utilised parts of earlier camp defences.

Knowledge of their location can be transmitted through the centuries and, despite landscape change, through place name evidence. In the eighteenth century, the camp at Kirkbuddo in Angus was known locally as 'Haerfauds', which means 'the ditches, trenches or folds of the "strangers"'. A seventeenth-century source refers to a Danish camp in the vicinity but it was not until the mid-eighteenth century that fieldwork by Robert Melville and William Roy (see Chapter 6) correctly identified the site as of Roman origin[11]. Although clearly in an excellent state of survival at that time, agricultural practices have resulted in the gradual reduction of the earthworks so that, now, part of the camp is only known through crop-markings from the air (Figure 37). However, the southern portion of the camp remains in an extremely good state of preservation thanks to its location in Whig Street Wood. At this point, the rampart survives up to a height of 1 m and is spread over 4.6 m in width, with a ditch some half a metre deep in places and well over 1 m wide (Plate 10). Other place names, which can help to indicate earlier landscape features, include Castledykes (in Lanarkshire), Battledykes (in Angus), Wardykes (now known as Keithock, in Angus), Campmuir (now known as Lintrose, in Perthshire) and Raedykes (in Aberdeenshire). Intriguingly, the camp of Arosfa Garreg in the Brecon Beacons

37. Aerial view of Kirkbuddo in Angus. © Crown Copyright: RCAHMS. SC357337. Licensor www.rcahms.gov.uk

in Carmarthenshire lies close to a low crest with the place name 'Bryn Elen'. Many Roman roads in Wales are locally named 'Sarn Helen' which, it has been postulated, could have come from Sarn-yr-leon meaning 'causeway of the legion'. The word 'Bryn' means 'hill' and it is therefore possible that 'Bryn Elen' means 'hill of the legion'[12].

The camp at Normandykes in Aberdeenshire was originally believed to date to the time of William the Conqueror, and certainly a military function was ascribed in local folklore. The majority of the camp lies in arable fields on a low ridge on the north side of the River Dee with much of the perimeter recorded as crop-markings from the air, but the eastern part of the north rampart and ditch survives as the north side of a plantation, accentuated by the superimposition of a plantation bank resulting in a very pronounced earthwork over 1.5 m high. A drain has been cut along the original line of the ditch. The western part of the north side lies under the stone dyke of a field wall (Figure 38). In arable areas, later drainage

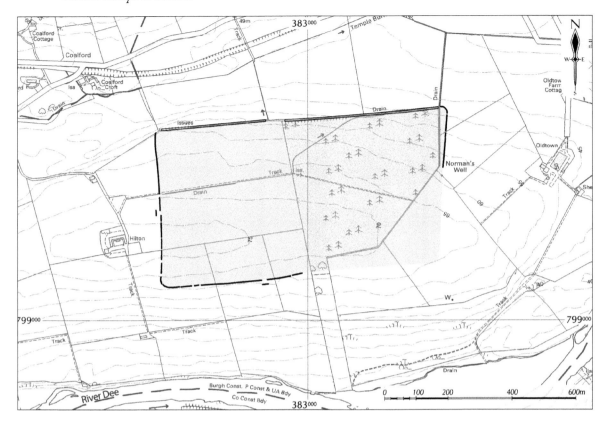

38. Plan of the camp of Normandykes in Aberdeenshire.

activity often utilised the pre-existing drain created by camp ditches. The rampart may also have been used for field boundaries, as appears to have been the case at Normandykes. Indeed, many camp perimeters have been utilised as field boundaries, which has preserved them to some extent when the rest of the area has been ploughed.

The fort of Castledykes in Lanarkshire is surrounded by a series of camps, probably from several different phases of campaigns in the area, and the fort has revealed, on excavation, evidence for having been occupied in both the first and second centuries AD. One of the camps lying immediately to the north of the fort (Figure 39) is one of the few examples of the physical residues of a site clearly being utilised by settlement a short while later, probably in the early historic/early medieval period. Here, a field system is visible through crop-markings, with linear crop-markings, pits, and sunken features reminiscent of *grübenhäuser* – semi-subterranean Anglo-Saxon houses found elsewhere in Britain and in northern Europe. The field system recorded here overlaps several of the camps in the area but part of it, including what appears to be a trackway, utilised the entrance of the camp north of the fort.

Short stretches of upstanding camp perimeter occasionally survive due to their re-use in the later landscape, but on only one occasion in Britain do presumably contemporary

39. Aerial view of one of the camps at Castledykes in Lanarkshire depicting the overlapping field system (and parts of other camps), taken from the south-east in 1984. Crown Copyright: RCAHMS. SC1164046. Licensor www.rcahms.gov.uk

internal features survive as upstanding remains, at Steeds Stalls (see Chapter 3). An examination of the maps made by the various antiquarians compared to the modern record indicates that almost 25 per cent of camps known before the start of the twentieth century have now had their surface traces obliterated by predominantly agricultural land-use in the intervening centuries, and a further 18 per cent have been reduced to partial earthworks.

Modern road layouts appear also to have been affected on occasion, but it is more common for these to have been influenced by the Roman roads which are sometimes located not far from the camps. At Muirhouses on the Antonine Wall in West Lothian, the minor road appears to bend to avoid the obstacle that the camp perimeter must have represented when the road developed (Figure 40), but on numerous other occasions stretches of camp ditch can be located on either side, suggesting modern roads may have occasionally utilised the camp entrances for their routes, giving an indication of the likely survival of earthwork remains at least until that road came into use. But elsewhere it appears that Roman camps were not significant obstacles to the construction of more modern roads, unlike forts, whose more substantial remains could sometimes affect the line of later roads.

The current evidence from both upstanding camps and crop-markings demonstrates that they stood, and in some areas still stand, in an evolving landscape, being utilised for a wide range of later enclosures and boundaries, including fields and plantations, with occasional roads changing alignment to avoid their perimeters. However, camps played a lesser role in

40. Aerial view of the camp of Muirhouses in West Lothian, taken from the south-west in 1996, showing the road bending around the south side of the camp. © Crown Copyright: RCAHMS. SC624718. Licensor www.rcahms.gov.uk

defining the later landscape than more dominant and long-lasting Roman features, such as Roman roads, which were probably still utilised as roads for a considerable period after the departure of the Roman army. For the Romans, leaving such structures in the landscape could provide defensive enclosures to be exploited by the local population. But the decision to slight a camp on departure does not appear to have been the normal procedure for the Roman army in Britain, leaving some of the substantial monuments that survive today, and whether the camps were considered to be tainted ground or were regarded as Roman territory is perhaps continued in local folklore. It is also unclear if they were left upstanding due to some form of treaty negotiation. Julius Frontinus (see Chapter 4) recorded in the first century AD that the Emperor Domitian compensated farmers in Germany for the loss of their crops when their lands were taken over for fortifications[13]. Undoubtedly their remains were testament to the might and power of the Roman army, in the same way that they are today.

8

Form: Defences, Gates
and Annexes

Thanks to the research detailed in Chapter 6, our knowledge of the archaeological remains of Roman temporary camps has expanded enormously since records were made of these structures in the eighteenth century. The interest of antiquarians, the explosion of information through aerial survey, recent developments in remote sensing, and modern excavations combine to give us a level of understanding of the form of these enclosures, occupied for a short time by Roman forces. This history of research enables us now to interpret many earthwork remains and crop-markings as those belonging to Roman camps without resorting to the spade, although recent excavations have furnished us with many more details regarding the physical construction of camps as well as recovering some features from their interiors. The survival of their perimeter defences, displaying standardised shapes, is the primary way in which we can identify camps, but particular forms of entrance protection and additional features such as annexes aid our understanding. Details of internal structures such as ovens and pits are now being interpreted through aerial photographs and excavation and provide glimpses into the daily lives of soldiers on the move.

DEFENCES

The significant elements of a Roman camp that enable them to be detected archaeologically are the enclosing rampart and ditch and any gate defences. If the camp was originally contained within defences that were slight or without a ditch, then little might survive to be detected today, particularly for those sites levelled by the plough. In addition, if such features as ramparts and ditches were not constructed at all and just flags or palisades employed, then the camp would be difficult to detect.

Camps are often first identified from the air through the regularity of the linear crop-markings, any evidence of protection for a gate or perhaps a change of alignment at an entrance break, and their rounded corners. Excavations can help to confirm identification and classification, although many have concentrated on the perimeter ditches and it is only in recent years that camp interiors have been investigated, enabling us to put some flesh on the bones of our knowledge.

When it comes to camp perimeter defences, the dimensions of both rampart and ditch vary considerably in terms of height, depth and width. On occasion, excavations have

41. View of the north-east corner of Arosfa Garreg in Carmarthenshire. Photograph taken in 1999.

identified ditches that have been cut through rock, representing a surprising amount of labour for something that was probably only occupied for a short period of time. It has already been observed that the ditch of the south camp at Burnswark in Dumfriesshire appears to have been cut through rock (Chapter 3) and excavations at Ward Law (also Dumfriesshire), Channelkirk (Scottish Borders) and Hillside Dunblane (Stirlingshire) all revealed evidence for rock-cut ditches[1]. Excavations through upstanding ramparts of camps have been rare, but when these have taken place they have demonstrated the use of turves, as proposed by ancient authors such as Vegetius[2] but peat, sand, earth, stones and clay have also been recorded, supporting Hyginus' statement that they use 'turf, stone, rocks or rubble'[3], depending on what was available for use locally.

The traces of upstanding rampart visible in the archaeological record give an indication of the massive and imposing nature of the camps, and can only begin to conjure up the visual reality and activity of a camp site occupied by thousands of troops housed in rows upon rows of tents with space for baggage, mules and other *impedimenta* (baggage) (see Chapter 5). At sites in upland areas of Wales, Northumberland and Scotland, the sheer scale of the rampart and ditch can begin to be appreciated (Plate 10 and Figure 41). Indeed, detailed topographic survey of many of the upstanding camps in England concluded that the rampart was the most important feature of the camp, with the ditch serving as additional defence[4]. This could help explain why we have significant gaps in our record for camps (see Figure 2), particularly in arable areas where ramparts have been destroyed by centuries of ploughing and the ditch was not constructed or was not of sufficient depth to either survive or provide strong enough recognisable crop-markings.

Vegetius emphasises the importance of the construction of the camp rampart by detailing it first, before noting that 'when the earth is too loose for it to be possible to cut out the turf like a brick [for the rampart], the ditch is dug in 'temporary style', 5 ft wide, 3 ft deep, with the rampart rising on the inside'[5]. Furthermore, he notes that deeper ditches should be dug 'when more serious forces of the enemy threaten'[6] but continues to reinforce the importance of the rampart and its revetments. Vegetius makes reference to 3-foot-high ramparts but Hyginus tells us that they should be 6 ft high and 8 ft wide[7] – these larger dimensions must have been employed at many of the camps in Britain due to the survival of the remains (with the ramparts at over a dozen camps surviving to a height of three Roman feet or more). Hyginus also informs us that in more secure places, 'the ditch is used for the sake of discipline', again reinforcing its secondary nature to the camp rampart[8].

One of the most remarkably preserved examples of camp ramparts in Britain is at Rey Cross in County Durham (see Figure 20), where the rampart survives up to 1.8 m high in places and measures as much as 11 m wide across its base[9]. At this camp, the ditch is barely apparent on the surface. The addition of other defensive features, such as timber breastworks or palisades, would serve to further heighten the rampart, leaving quite a dominant visual spectacle (Plate 11). Additional defences for camps on top of ramparts are attested in classical literature[10], but leave little or no archaeological trace. Both Livy and Vegetius refer to a palisade atop the rampart[11], and it has been suggested that the so-called *pilum murale* (or *pila muralia*, double-pointed wooden stakes) found at the fort of Great Chesters on Hadrian's Wall and elsewhere could have been used to form some an additional defence around a temporary camp (Figure 42)[12]. The provision of a central 'grip' or 'waist' in the middle of these sharpened stakes (also called *valli*) has given rise to the suggestion that they could have been lashed together in the form of a caltrop (Plate 12), but it would equally have made them easier to carry. They were also sharpened at both ends and could have pointed out towards the enemy rather than just have been lashed together as a palisade. A strong palisade placed somewhere on the rampart of a camp would be expected to leave a trace in the upstanding remains where these survive to a sufficient height, although there has not been enough excavation or other detailed analysis to test this. Possible stake holes have been excavated at the entrances to a couple of camps in Scotland (Castledykes in Lanarkshire and Dalginross in Perthshire), and these may hint at additional contemporary defensive features. Evidence of stakes along the forward face of the bank was also tentatively identified at Galley Gill in Cumbria[13]. If caltrops were used, these might only rest on the surface, leaving the archaeological evidence slight or non-existent. Hyginus refers to five possible types of camp fortifications: ditch, rampart, stakes, stockade and weapons[14], and goes on to state that the use of these depends on the location and availability of various building and defensive materials.

Evidence for the ditches of camps is varied, and we have seen from the sources that ditches may not have been required at all camps, making them harder to detect unless the ramparts survive in earthwork form. In addition, camps regularly exhibit quite different sized ditches from one side to the other. This is likely to be partially due to survival across the millennia, but could represent real choices made during their construction; after all, if it is possible to mix banks with palisades around the perimeter of a camp (see Chapter 3), differences in the scale of ditches should not surprise us. Furthermore, not every group of troops might construct their sector of rampart and ditch identically to the next group, and

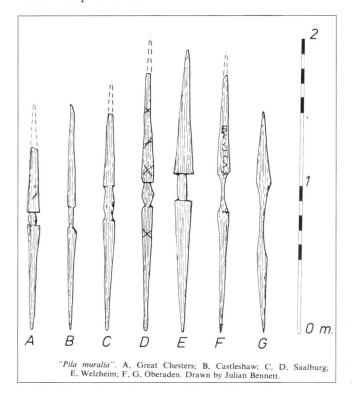

"*Pila muralia*". A, Great Chesters; B, Castleshaw; C, D, Saalburg; E, Welzheim; F, G, Oberaden. Drawn by Julian Bennett.

42. Stakes found at Great Chesters on Hadrian's Wall, drawn by Julian Bennett. (Reproduced *Archaeologia Aeliana* 1982)

the ground conditions will naturally play a significant part. At the camp of Craigarnhall in Stirlingshire, excavations on four separate occasions revealed considerable variance in the ditch from 1.5 m to 3 m in width and from 0.4 m to 1.5 m in depth[15]. Although this can be partly explained by differing survival rates, the lack of uniformity may also be due to the work of different units, the nature of the subsoil, and possibly the perceived threat to one of the sides if it benefited from additional natural defences.

The irregularly shaped camp at Raedykes in Aberdeenshire (Figure 43) has the largest ditch so far excavated, perhaps unsurprising given that the rampart and ditch remain significant earthwork features, with the rampart spread about 5 m wide in places and up to 1 m in height. Excavations in 1914 identified that the ditch was V-shaped, about 4.5 m wide and 2.1 m deep, and faced in places with puddled clay up to 5 cm thick. Interestingly, where the ditch was smaller, the rampart was also smaller. This was used to argue that lesser dimensions were employed in areas on the camp where the ground rendered an attack from that angle unlikely[16] but survival rates must also be a factor.

Elsewhere, camp ditches have quite a varied survival rate and, in some instances, the defences have survived due to their incorporation into later landscape features (see Chapter 7). Excavations at one of the camps at Lochlands in Stirlingshire revealed only the remains of the base of the ditch, the rest presumably having been ploughed away; the crop-marking of the ditch was only occasionally visible on air photographs and the degraded remains explain why it proved so elusive.

43. Vertical air photograph of the camp at Raedykes, taken by the Ordnance Survey in 1965. The four sides of the camp are indicated by arrows. © Crown Copyright: RCAHMS OS Collection: OS/65/028_0127

Corners of camps are usually rounded because the creation of a sharp angle would present a constructional weak point and be easier to destroy, particularly if it was built of turf, and it has been observed in masonry structures that rounded corners are easier to build when using unskilled labour[17]. Hyginus stated that the corners should be at an angle of 90 degrees[18], but this is evidentially not always adhered to. A gently rounded angle avoids a sharp point which could be easier to attack, and also provides additional defence in terms of the number of men who could be employed on a curved as opposed to a pointed perimeter corner.

Caesar makes reference to an *ericus*, a beam studded with spikes in front of the entrance[19]. Whether or not an *ericus* deployed across an entrance would leave traces in the archaeological record depends on how it was placed into the ground. There is no obvious evidence for such, although occasional additional slight ditches are known across entrance gaps (for example, at Eskbank in Midlothian) which could have been trenches for temporary hurdling or the deployment of an *ericus*, although equally could relate to drainage[20]. It seems unlikely that the Romans would have carried an *ericus* around with them, but perhaps one could have been constructed on site, provided that suitable materials could be located.

Caesar also reported that he utilised large forked branches above the palisade of his siege camp at Alesia, and dug *lilia* (defensive pits) in front[21]. Forked branches and other brushwood could also have been used to provide additional defences around a camp and hawthorn has been found buried in the ditches of more permanent structures (for example, in a possible camp under the Roman fort at Bar Hill on the Antonine Wall[22]). No evidence has been

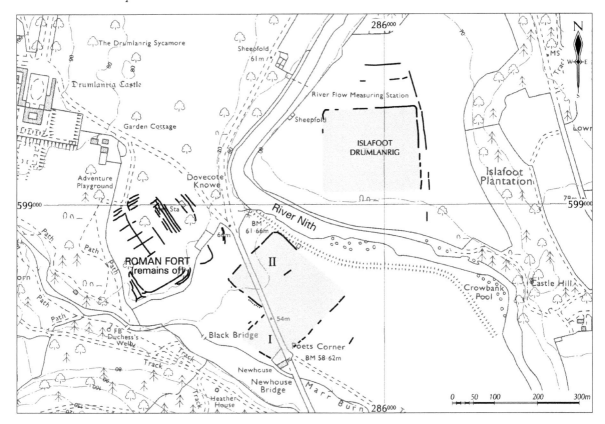

44. Plan of the camps at Drumlanrig in Dumfriesshire, showing the possible line of pits outside the south-west side of camp II.

uncovered for any *lilia* although, admittedly, there have been very few excavations of areas outside temporary camps. Pits are visible on air photographs at some sites, but their date and function is unknown. Certainly, there is no evidence from air photographs of defensive pits constructed outside a camp in the regular manner of those known in front of Hadrian's Wall and the Antonine Wall, although a regular line of pits is clearly visible on air photographs outside the west side of one of the camps at Drumlanrig in Dumfriesshire (Figure 44). The labour expended in the construction of the camp was presumably enough for a temporary occupation without digging such extra features unless extreme circumstances prevailed.

SHAPES

Roman camps are usually square or rectangular in shape, with some occasionally deviating from the norm, often due to topographical factors. Vegetius commented that once the campsite had been selected, the camp could be built 'square, circular or triangular'[23]; circular and triangular camps are not known in Britain, but perhaps if any were visible, they might not have been identified as Roman in date.

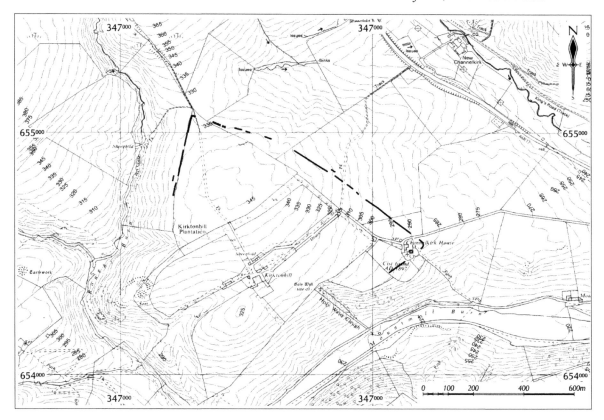

45. Plan of the camp of Channelkirk, Scottish Borders.

At Channelkirk in the Scottish Borders, adjacent to the Dere Street Roman road, parts of three sides of an extremely large camp have been recorded as either earthworks or through crop-markings since the eighteenth century. The camp was clearly extremely large and enclosed at least 47 hectares (117 acres) and may have enclosed somewhere in the region of 66 hectares (165 acres – see Chapter 9), but it was irregular in shape (Figure 45). In the mid-eighteenth century, William Roy (see Chapter 6) thought that it ran to a small earthwork now interpreted as an Iron Age fort. Although the line that Roy found has not been confirmed, if the camp perimeter ran close to his suggested line then it would have been almost triangular in form.

Other unusually shaped camps in Britain, such as Twyn-y-briddallt in Glamorgan (Figure 16), Cawthorn in North Yorkshire, Milestone House in Northumberland, Plumpton Head in Cumbria, and Raedykes in Aberdeenshire (Figure 43), can sometimes be explained by their topography or the avoidance of an existing structure such as a permanent fort. Certainly there is a broad range of shapes, particularly among the larger camps, where availability of suitable ground would have taken precedence over conforming to a particular form[24]. Occasionally, projecting corners have been observed on camps, but not always explained due to the surrounding topography (for example, at Innerpeffray East in

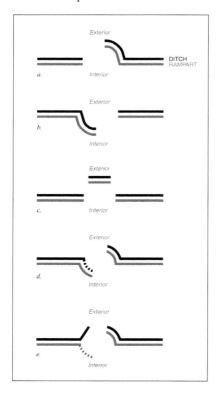

46. Schematic drawing of different types of entrance protection in use on camps in Britain. a. external *clavicula*; b. internal *clavicula*; c. *titulus*; d. cuspate entrance; e. Stracathro-type gate. © Crown Copyright: RCAHMS. Licensor www.rcahms.gov.uk

Perthshire, see Figure 61). Corners represent weak points on the circuit, and the acute angles created by this feature would have been harder to defend, but it is possible that they served to funnel any camp visitors towards the main entrance to the camp (the *porta praetoria*). Elsewhere, the defensive perimeters of camps sometimes change direction at their gates. This is again sometimes for topographic reasons. Such changes of alignment can therefore help to predict gate location.

The internal layouts of slightly irregular camps must have been adjusted to suit their perimeters, but continuation of internal symmetry can usually be observed from the location of the side gates, which oppose one another (see Chapter 5).

GATES

The entrances to a camp represented defensive weak points on the circuit, and it should be expected that these would be kept to a minimum without impeding the ability of the army encamped inside to go about its business. If a camp were to be occupied for several days or weeks, it might be expected that access in and out of the camp would be an important element to consider during its construction. A typical camp, according to Hyginus, was provided with six entrances, but across Britain, numbers of gates range from one (Gallaberry in Dumfriesshire, see Chapter 6) to ten or eleven (Rey Cross in County Durham, see Chapter 4, and Crackenthorpe in Cumbria[25]).

Differing types of entrance protection were employed at camps in Britain and across the Empire (Figure 46). The most common known is the *titulus* (plural: *tituli*) – a short stretch of rampart and ditch, set forward from the entrance gap, providing an obstacle to be navigated by all camp entrants. Across Britain, some 45 per cent of camps exhibit evidence for *tituli* at their entrances. Another gate form is the *clavicula* (plural: *claviculae*) – a semi-circular rampart constructed to expose the unshielded side of those entering the camp to the defenders. In contrast to the commonality of *tituli*, less than 9 per cent of camps in Britain have revealed evidence for *claviculae*, but many of these are only known from upstanding earthworks, and only recorded through archaeological crop-markings when accompanied by curved ditches, which does not appear to have been routine (and it seems likely that many *claviculae* ramparts were destroyed through centuries of ploughing). Only a handful of camps appear to have had this internal *clavicula* rampart accompanied by an internal ditch, thereby leaving a stronger archaeological footprint. This has been the case at crop-mark sites such as Norton Fitzwarren in Somerset and Newton on Trent in Lincolnshire[26]. Other recorded examples of internal ditched *claviculae* include Dargues in Northumberland, where the internal *clavicula* ditch can still be seen on the ground, and one of the camps at Troutbeck in Cumbria, where the ditch following the internal *clavicula* on the south-east side of the camp was recorded through excavation[27]. Double *claviculae*, known as 'cuspate' gates, are also occasionally recorded, including at the other two camps at Troutbeck in Cumbria and at Oakwood in the Scottish Borders[28]. Occasionally, ditches may have accompanied external *claviculae* ramparts. This was the case at the well-preserved example of Cawthorn C in North Yorkshire, an unusually shaped camp with three external *clavicula* ramparts and ditches visible on one side[29] (Plate 13). Furthermore, ditched external *claviculae* are visible as crop-markings at Milrighall in the Scottish Borders and at Hoole, outside Chester[30]. Whether these sites also had internal *claviculae* ramparts it is no longer possible to say. External *claviculae* are generally rare in Britain, with only a few examples currently known, but are recorded elsewhere in the Empire, for example at Tell Abara in Jordan, Nahal Hever in Israel and Qasr Ibrim in Egypt[31].

The main example of curved ditches accompanying *claviculae* ramparts are in the variant form of gates known as the Stracathro-type (named after the site in Angus where the phenomenon was first observed by St Joseph from the air in the 1950s). These consist of an external *clavicula* rampart and ditch with an oblique ditch (possibly accompanied by a rampart, although none are known) guarding the entrance gap (Figures 46 and 47). It was also probably accompanied by an internal curving rampart (without a ditch). These are rarely recorded and currently only found in Scotland.

Simple entrance gaps are recorded at almost 23 per cent of camps across Britain, and not enough of the camp is recorded to have any confidence of the gate location or type for a further 18 per cent (Figure 48). It is possible, therefore, that *claviculae* may have been in more predominant use, but the majority are only recorded from upstanding camps and many more may not have survived to tell their story.

Permanent forts rarely deployed the same elaborate entrance protection as camps, although in-turned ramparts and ditches are known from a number of sites. A rare exception is the fort of Bar Hill on the Antonine Wall in Dunbartonshire, which has

47. Aerial view of the south-east gate at the eponymous type-site of Stracathro in Angus, taken from the west in 1979. © Crown Copyright: RCAHMS. SC1164182. Licensor www.rcahms.gov.uk

ditched *tituli* at two of its gates. The well-preserved earthwork fort of Ardoch in Perthshire also possesses a curious curved ditch on its eastern side which is attached to one of the outer ditches of the fort. This feature has been interpreted as either a *clavicula* ditch or an earlier *titulus* which was incorporated into a later phase of the camp ditches[32].

It has already been noted that the *titulus* was most common gate form in use in Britain, on the basis of our current archaeological knowledge. Camps with *tituli* are also known from across the Roman Empire from the Netherlands to Romania. At El Pedrosillo in southern Spain, over a hundred *tituli* are recorded forming freestanding obstacles and this unique evidence has been interpreted as a probable battlefield site[33]. Probably the earliest recorded examples from camps are in Spain, at the siege works near Numantia (in the second and first century BC[34]). Several of the practice camps in Wales exhibit *tituli*, particularly those around the forts of Tomen-y-Mur in Merioneth and Castell Collen in

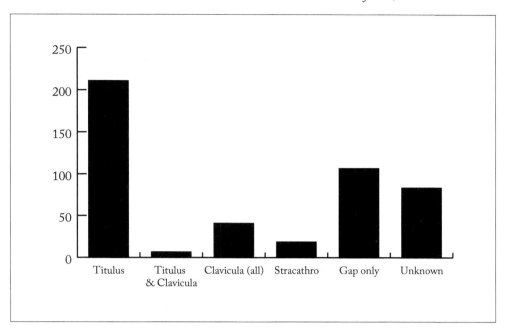

48. Table of camp entrances.

Radnorshire[35]. No *tituli* are recorded on Trajan's Column, but this may be because they were difficult to illustrate clearly. *Tituli* appear to have been deployed for entrance protection from the second century BC through to the later part of the Roman Empire. Few *tituli* have been excavated, but one of the camps at Lochlands in Stirlingshire produced a *denarius* coin of Hadrian in the upper fill of its ditch, and sherds from a pottery bowl, probably dating to the mid-second century AD, were recovered from the fill of the *titulus* ditch at Dunning in Perthshire[36].

Upstanding earthwork *tituli* are rare and have only been recorded at a handful of sites, including Battledykes, at Oathlaw in Angus (see Chapter 6), where a single *titulus* is the only earthwork surviving in a camp now largely visible as crop-markings (Figure 27). One of the most bizarre arrangements of *tituli* is at Ward Law in Dumfriesshire. This camp, first recorded as an earthwork in the eighteenth century, is now only known through crop-markings from the air. On its northern gate, the entrance gap is protected by four *tituli* in an apparent diamond-shaped arrangement (Figure 49). There are no parallels for such a gateway anywhere else in Britain and it has been suggested that there may have been a training element in the construction of so many obstacles at a single gate. In contrast, excavations and geophysical survey failed to find a *titulus* at one of the other entrances, but a third has a single *titulus*[37]. Thus it appears that the utilisation of the same entrance protection throughout a camp may not have been a pre-requisite.

One final, curious feature of Ward Law is that there appears to be an outwork connecting the camp to a local hill-fort to the south. This additional ditch, only known through crop-markings, also displays an entrance gap protected by a *titulus*, but any other connection

49. Aerial view of multiple *tituli* at the north-west gate at Ward Law in Dumfriesshire, taken from the north-east in 1984. © Crown Copyright: RCAHMS. SC360860. Licensor www.rcahms.gov.uk

between the occupations of camp and hill-fort is unclear. If the camp were involved in the training of troops, this might be one explanation for these additional features, although extending the camp to the hill-fort does take in the nearby hill which overlooked the confluence of the Nith and Solway.

Hyginus refers to the use of a *titulus* or *titulum* at gateways, but refers to this gate defence in tandem with an internal *clavicula*[38] (Figure 46). The use of both *claviculae* and *tituli* at the same entrance has only been recorded on a handful of camps, such as Chapel Rig and Glenwhelt Leazes, two neighbouring camps on Hadrian's Wall in Northumberland[39], and also at a few sites further afield (for example, in Romania at Comārnicel and Vârful lui Petru[40]). Use of *claviculae* could have been far more ubiquitous, with many potentially destroyed by the plough, particularly if they were only in rampart form and were not accompanied by a curving ditched element. Different entrance types on the same camp are

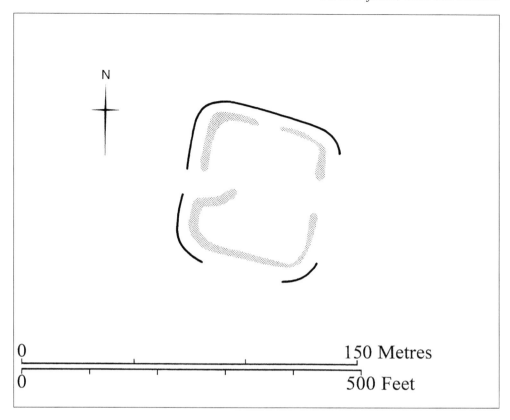

N

| 0 | 150 Metres |
| 0 | 500 Feet |

50. Drawing of the practice camp of Gelligaer Common II in Glamorgan.

recorded on occasion, such as at Bellshiel in Northumberland, where the camp possesses a *titulus* at one gate and a *clavicula* at another[41].

The majority of surviving upstanding camps with internal *claviculae* lie in Northumberland and in parts of upland Wales, the two areas in Britain where Roman camps are best preserved. In Wales, they are recorded on a number of practice camps, most notably on the common west of the forts at Gelligaer in Glamorgan[42]. One of these camps, Gelligaer Common II, is reasonably well preserved in rough pasture and rectangular in shape, measuring about 33 m by 29 m (Figure 50). The rampart survives to a height of almost 1 m in places and the ditch can also be traced on the ground. On one side the camp possesses an internal *clavicula*, which survives to a height of about 0.4 m and is spread about 3.5 m in width[43]. Some 2 km to the south-east lies the fort of Gelligaer, which was constructed in the late first century AD; it was subsequently abandoned sometime in the early second century AD when a smaller, stone fort was built a short distance away.

When it comes to Stracathro-type camps, although these are first fully named from their aerial discovery in the 1950s, one of the camps with this unusual form of entrance protection, that at Dalginross in Perthshire, was first recorded and planned in earthwork form by William Roy (see Chapter 6) in 1755 (Figure 51)[44]. He recorded its unusual gateways,

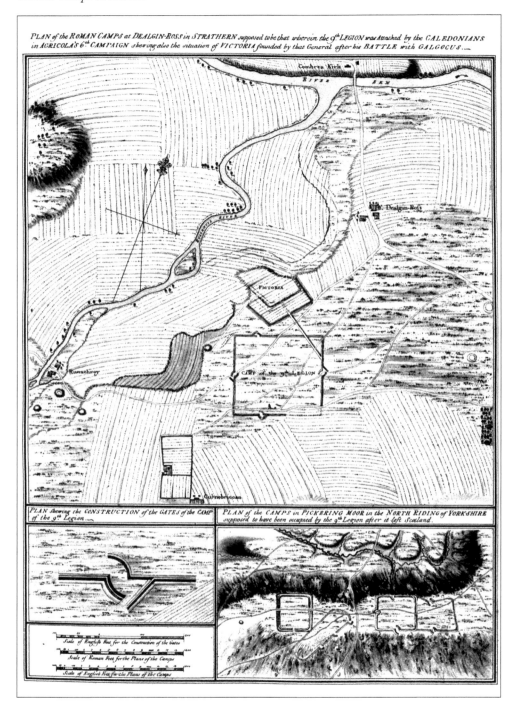

51. Plan of the fort and camp at Dalginross in Perthshire, made by William Roy in 1755. (Plate XI from 'Military Antiquities of the Romans in Britain'). © Courtesy of RCAHMS (Society of Antiquaries of London). SC1164071. Licensor www.rcahms.gov.uk

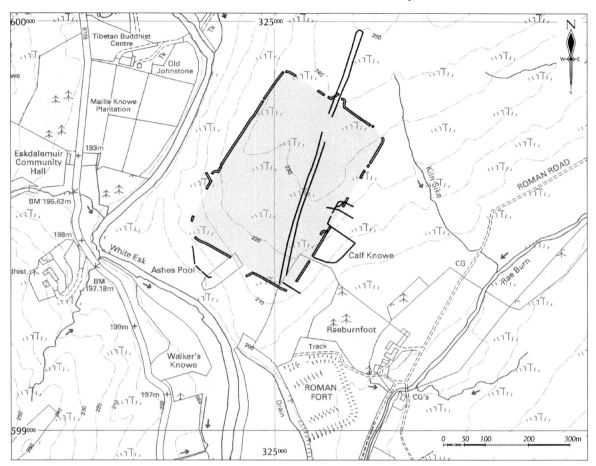

52. Plan of the camp of Raeburnfoot in Dumfriesshire.

comparing them to those on the camps at Cawthorn in North Yorkshire (Chapter 9 and Plate 13). In the intervening few centuries, the camp has been ploughed out and is now only known through crop-markings visible on air photographs (Plate 14). The entrances on all four sides have been recorded from the air and all possess the unusual defensive outworks known as the 'Stracathro-type'. Excavations on the eastern gate of the camp suggested that its ditches had been backfilled with turves prior to re-cutting, possibly indicating deliberate slighting on abandonment. A post-hole recorded just inside the re-cut *clavicula* could have held a stake pushed into the bank[45]. A series of pits is visible in the interior of the camp, probably rubbish pits indicating the locations of the rows of tents[46].

Another 'Stracathro-type' camp is known at Raeburnfoot in Dumfriesshire, and was only first discovered in 2004[47]. Although still surviving in earthwork form (it is the only example of a camp with 'Stracathro-type' gates to survive as an earthwork), the remains are significantly denuded, which is why it escaped detection for so long, despite being sited on moorland close to a Roman fort. The camp appears to have possessed four entrances – two displayed external *claviculae* ramparts and accompanying oblique ditches, but no internal *claviculae* could be found (Figure 52), despite topographic survey and detailed contour modelling, which has enabled better understanding of the camp's very slight remains (Plate 15). However, on one side, an earthwork feature has survived which is strongly suggestive of an internal *clavicula*. The camp rampart does not appear to break for an entrance at this point, but the camp in this area has been disturbed by later field banks and enclosures, and the ground outside the likely entrance has been scarped, removing any signs of an external *clavicula* and oblique ditch. It therefore seems likely that some of the gates also possessed internal *claviculae*, but that those elsewhere have eroded and are no longer detectable on the ground. Their absence at the other gates may be genuine, although the survival of the earthwork of this camp is so poor that they could have eroded. Any traces of internal *claviculae* banks at Dalginross and at all other Stracathro-type camps have been obliterated through ploughing.

INTERNAL FEATURES

Thus far, concentration has been placed on the perimeters of Roman camps – the features that enable them to be detected and interpreted. But this does not help us to understand how camps were used and what they were like to inhabit for the soldiers stationed within. Unlike forts, where timber and stone structures and artefactual and environmental evidence can help to build a picture of the Roman military life, our understanding of the life of soldiers on the move is far less developed. Until recently, camps were commonly believed to be largely devoid of archaeological features because of their transient occupation. Focus has been given to their perimeters, which have occasionally yielded artefacts, such as pottery, enabling dates to be proposed. One camp with clear internal structures is the presumed construction camp at Steeds Stalls in Perthshire (see Chapter 3 and Figure 9), where the internal features may represent the remains of lime-kilns, possibly connected to the construction of the nearby fortress of Inchtuthil.

But, as discussed in Chapter 5, marching camps accommodated many thousands of men and their accompanying horses, baggage and mules. These soldiers, housed in leather tents (Plate 16), would have required places for cooking (hearths and ovens), latrines, and general rubbish pits. The length of time during which a camp was occupied is unknown and no doubt would have varied greatly depending on the circumstances of occupation and the purpose of the camp. It might be expected that construction camps (see Chapter 3) would have housed troops for a longer period than normal and, therefore, be more likely to provide evidence for internal settlement. However, in the limited excavations on the presumed construction camps along the Antonine Wall, few internal features have been found[48]. At siege camps, where the occupation may also have extended over a protracted period, greater information on internal structures has been recorded elsewhere in the Empire, particularly at camps such as Masada in Israel (Figure 1), where the main construction material was stone. Interior features of camps could give clues as to their function, and it is arguable that more features should be expected from those sites which had a longer period of occupation.

Excavations in camp interiors have occasionally revealed areas of cobbling or paving. This was noted during nineteenth-century excavations at Burnswark in Dumfriesshire (see Chapter 3) but not located during later investigations. Elsewhere, light cobbling and posthole depressions were identified at Hillside Annan (also Dumfriesshire), and cobbling and burning were discovered in a structure that may have had temporary occupation under the fort at Bar Hill on the Antonine Wall (see Chapter 3). Small exploratory trenches in camp interiors elsewhere frequently fail to locate any features, but this may be as much to do with the small-scale nature of excavations which have hitherto been conducted on camp interiors. The principal exception to this is the camp at Kintore in Aberdeenshire, which has revealed a wealth of internal features during large-scale excavations (see below), although small-scale excavations on the interiors of other camps (such as Normandykes, also Aberdeenshire[49], and Bromfield in Shropshire [see below]) has recorded features likely to be contemporary with the Roman occupation of these camps. At the camps at Ardoch in Perthshire (also see Chapter 9), the surviving upstanding rampart of one camp was slighted at various points which coincided with the likely locations of street lines for a later camp[50]. This signifies the importance of internal access across the camps and the use and maintenance of the internal street system (see Chapter 5).

With the exception of the cobbling and possible structure at Burnswark South in Dumfriesshire, proposed during excavations in the 1890s but not identified excavations in the 1960s (see Chapter 3), internal buildings are not known from camps, with accommodation provided by leather tents. Indeed, were a building to be identified within a temporary camp then the site's status would probably be changed from camp to fort, recognising that a more permanent occupation was presumably intended. At Kintore (see below), a four-post structure was excavated, which was argued to be a Roman watch-tower overlooking a gap in the perimeter ditch for a palaeochannel, but there was no supporting dating evidence and the evidence for its interpretation as Roman in date is tenuous. One of the rare occasions when more permanent structures were built is highlighted during Caesar's campaigns in Gaul, when he makes reference to his troops constructing and thatching shelters over the tents during a winter campaign[51]. However, it is generally believed that campaigns in Britain were conducted during the summer months and no such provision would have been necessary. The only exception to this might be the possibility that some permanent forts started life as temporary camps with shelters constructed over the tents when they were occupied for a longer period, as discussed earlier, in which case their identification as temporary camps would be difficult (see Chapter 3).

Ovens and Pits

One type of feature, which has occasionally been revealed through excavations of camp interiors, is the Roman oven (Plates 17 and 18). Bipartite ovens (Figure 53) are by far the most common type recorded, and consist of two parts, often in a figure-of-eight or keyhole pattern, usually forming an oven pit and stoke hole. On more permanent structures such as forts and fortlets, ovens are often located in the *intervallum* space close to the perimeter. At the camps at Inchtuthil in Perthshire (see Chapter 5), the pits visible on air photographs located close to the ditch are slightly elongated hollows reminiscent of ovens and are usually interpreted as such, although none have yet been excavated (Figures 21 and 54). Other pits within the interior of these camps were excavated and interpreted as rubbish pits related to rows of tents[52]. The presence of ovens can sometimes provide material suitable for radiocarbon dating, and this technique has been applied at a number of sites, although, as a result, some ovens have produced later dates, suggesting that the ovens were used after the departure of the Roman army. Whether these actually indicate post-Roman activity by the local communities or problems with the samples obtained cannot be ascertained without further corroborating evidence. But bipartite ovens are known from a number of Iron Age sites and the design was not the exclusive copyright of the Roman army as they do represent an efficient construction for a cooking oven. For example, at Melville Nurseries, some 500 m west of the Flavian fort at Elginhaugh in Midlothian, two bipartite pits dating to the Roman period were excavated and are of very similar character to Roman military ovens[53]. A similar structure is recorded close to a souterrain (an Iron Age subterranean chamber or passage) at Cowiehall Quarry, east of Bannockburn[54].

Roman ovens are recorded from a handful of sites, most notably at Kintore in Aberdeenshire (see below). At Bromfield in Shropshire no fewer than four figure-of-eight ovens were excavated, comprising an oven itself with a firing/raking chamber. The ovens probably had dome roofs, and part of a collapsed clay dome was found in one oven at Bromfield[55]. Ovens would have been fired regularly, mainly for the purpose of baking bread. Associated plant remains at Bromfield included unidentified charred cereal seeds and three possible bread fragments. It is not known how frequently they were fired, but it is likely to have ranged between daily and weekly. At both Bromfield and Kintore there is evidence for more than one firing, which may indicate that the camp was not merely an overnight halting place. Clues to this have been provided through multiple ash lines visible in the raking chambers. If the ash pits were regularly cleaned out, the ash lines and deposits would not leave archaeological traces and our knowledge of their length of use would remain unknown, so we are fortunate that the soldiers occupying Bromfield and Kintore were not fastidious in cleaning their ovens after use.

Excavations at camps at Lochlands, Three Bridges in Stirlingshire recorded a number of pits, some of which were proposed as ovens or possibly even kilns, and it may have been the case that the camps here, close to the fort of Camelon and just north of the Antonine Wall, may have had a semi-industrial purpose relating to the construction and occupation of the Wall[56].

Pits and ovens are occasionally observed (usually from air photographs) outside camp perimeters. At Inchtuthil, outside the camps and the fortress, numerous pits are visible (Figures 21 and 54). It is possible that these are part of a larger enclosed area on the Inchtuthil plateau, potentially indicating a further stage of occupation of the plateau, or indicating the presence of camp followers. This could be one of the very few times when camp followers, usually largely ignored or invisible in the archaeological record, could possibly be detected (see Chapter 5). Elongated pits outside camps are also known in a few other locations, including Glenlochar in Dumfries & Galloway (see below). Some of these pits located outside camps may relate to additional defensive features, such as the *lilia* reported by Caesar at Alesia[57].

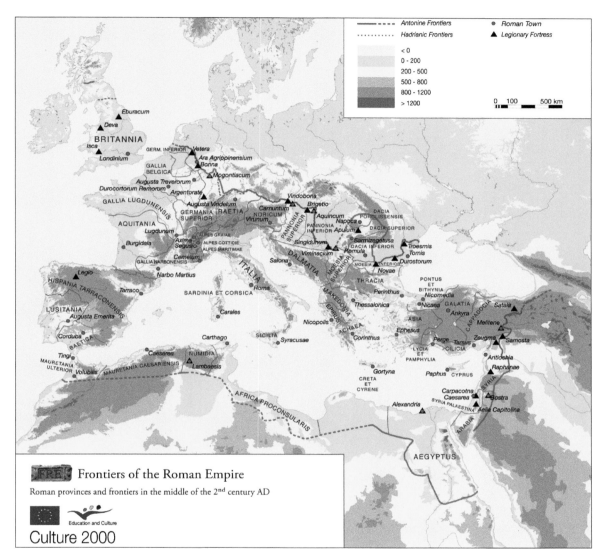

Legend:
Antonine Frontiers
Hadrianic Frontiers
Roman Town
Legionary Fortress

< 0
0 - 200
200 - 500
500 - 800
800 - 1200
> 1200

0   100   500 km

Frontiers of the Roman Empire

Roman provinces and frontiers in the middle of the 2nd century AD

Education and Culture

Culture 2000

1. Map of the Roman Empire. Created by Andrea Faber, Heinz-Jürgen Köhler and Kurt Schaller as part of the Frontiers of the Roman Empire project, funded by the European Union's Culture 2000 programme.

2. Aerial view across to Bennachie in Aberdeenshire. © Crown Copyright: RCAHMS. SC872649. Licensor www.rcahms.gov.uk

3. View of one of the siege camps at Numantia (Peña Redonda) in north-west Spain. Photograph taken in 2006.

4. Aerial view of the Roman construction camp at Tamfourhill, on the Antonine Wall in Stirlingshire. ©
Crown Copyright: RCAHMS. SC908888. Licensor www.rcahms.gov.uk

5. Aerial view of the Antonine Wall camps at Dullatur in Lanarkshire, under excavation in 1998. © Crown Copyright: RCAHMS. SC872940. Licensor www.rcahms.gov.uk

6. Reconstruction of a *groma* from Carnuntum in Austria. Photograph taken in 2005.

7. Photograph of Trajan's Column in Rome. Photograph taken in 2006.

8. Aerial view of the marching camp at Hindwell Farm in Radnorshire. © Crown Copyright: Royal Commission on the Ancient and Historical Monuments of Wales. 895504.15.

Opposite above: **9.** LiDAR image of the new camp at Carrawburgh, lying to the south-west of the Carrawburgh fort (Latin: Brocolitia) on Hadrian's Wall. © English Heritage; LiDAR source Cambridge University Unit for Landscape Modelling (March 2004).

Opposite below: **10.** View of a section of upstanding rampart and ditch surviving in Whig Street Wood at Kirkbuddo in Angus. Photograph taken in 2004.

11. View of a reconstructed palisade on top of a marching camp rampart, Carnuntum, Austria. Photograph taken in 2005.

Opposite above: **12.** View of a reconstruction of a section of the defences of a Roman marching camp with a 'caltrop' palisade at Archaeolink Prehistory Park, Aberdeenshire. Photograph taken in 2004.

Opposite below: **13.** View of one of the external *clavicula* gates of the camp at Cawthorn in North Yorkshire. Photograph taken in 2009.

Above: **14.** Aerial view of the camp at Dalginross in Perthshire. © Crown Copyright: RCAHMS. SC624586. Licensor www.rcahms.gov.uk

Left: **15.** Detailed three-dimensional contour model of the north-west gate at Raeburnfoot, surveyed using a differential Global Positioning System and with a x3 exaggeration. © Crown Copyright: RCAHMS. Licensor www.rcahms.gov.uk

16. View of a reconstructed tent from Archaeolink Prehistory Park, Aberdeenshire. Photograph taken in 2004.

17. View of a reconstructed Roman oven from the Saalburg in Germany. Photograph taken in 2004.

18. View of a reconstructed Roman oven from Archaeolink Prehistory Park, Aberdeenshire. Photograph taken in 2004.

19. Aerial view of the camp at Dun in Perthshire. © Crown Copyright: RCAHMS. DP050510. Licensor www.rcahms.gov.uk

20. Aerial view of the Roman fort at Ardoch in Perthshire, taken from the north under snow cover in 1984. © Crown Copyright: RCAHMS. SC337315. Licensor www.rcahms.gov.uk

21. Aerial view of the Roman fort and camps at Newstead, taken from the north-east in 2006. © Crown Copyright: RCAHMS. DP019895. Licensor www.rcahms.gov.uk

53. View of a bipartite oven from the excavations at Kintore in Aberdeenshire. © AOC Archaeology Group, ref. O087.

54. Aerial view of the pits running inside one of the camps at Inchtuthil in Perthshire. © Crown Copyright: RCAHMS. SC958608. Licensor www.rcahms.gov.uk

Ditched small features, which are presumably pits of some description, are frequently recorded on air photographs of Roman camps, but their contemporaneity with the occupation of the camp can rarely be proven. It is only when a level of regularity in their layout can be seen, such as the rows of pits visible at Dalginross and Inchtuthil in Perthshire (see Plate 14 and Figures 21 and 54), and at Moss Side in Cumbria, that a level of confidence as to their Roman attribution can be accepted, but the camp of Kintore is an exception to this, with very limited regularity in the Roman ovens and pits excavated in the interior (see below). Some 'pits' visible through crop-markings, such as those close to the perimeter of Inchtuthil, could be the remains of ovens.

Pits are visible within numerous camps, often scattered across their interiors with no obvious consistency, leaving their interpretation as Roman pits contemporary with the occupation of the camp as questionable. Occasionally, pits are clustered in a particular area and, if Roman in date, could indicate demarcation of that segment of the camp for activities which required the excavation of pits (whether latrines, rubbish-pits, cooking hollows and ovens, or concerned with the upkeep of horses and mules). At Carronbridge in Dumfriesshire, excavations located an oven outside the camp, and also revealed irregular post-holes just inside the entrance, each containing charred emmer wheat[58]. The purpose of these post-holes is unknown, but they could have had a cooking function or been involved in a fence line which may have demarcated an area for winnowing or some other such function.

The dating of pits has been problematic. Radiocarbon assays often provide a wide date range, although they can be used to tie evidence down to the general Roman period. Any artefacts recovered from camps need to have secure contexts. While the narrow timescale of occupation of camps may make some of the broad date ranges produced through radiocarbon dating close to useless, such dates, combined with other evidence, such as stratified artefacts, can aid in suggestions of contemporaneity and thus the analysis and interpretation of sites.

Kintore

Extensive excavations at the Roman camp of Kintore in Aberdeenshire since 2000 (and several smaller excavations prior to that date) have revealed a wealth of internal features and helped to paint a more rounded picture of the life of soldiers on the move. Some 180 bipartite ovens (Figure 53) are now known from the site, along with at least sixty rubbish pits and a plethora of non-Roman features[59]. The Roman ovens are scattered throughout much of the interior of the camp, with little obvious formal organisation or symmetry excepting one area where four irregular lines can possibly be identified. Others have been located where they would have traditionally been expected – within the *intervallum* area, tucked into the back of the rampart.

At various places in the camp, some of the ovens sit alongside one another and others cut through their neighbours, providing evidence for more than one phase of activity (or at least a period of repair and re-build), although the time gap between the two cannot at present be ascertained. Some appear to be 'double-ovens', with two cooking ends sharing a single ash pit. There is also considerable variability in styles (stone and cobble lined and unlined cooking pits), orientation and size of the ovens, some of which no doubt reflect their location and survival patterns, but also intriguingly possibly indicate different units and the different backgrounds of serving soldiers[60].

One of the ovens at Kintore produced burnt fragments of alder, and many of the others had charcoal fragments from oak, hazel, ash, elm and birch. Some of the remains could relate to the timber used in the construction of the oven, others fuel for burning. Some of the wood may have come from the burning of disused wooden structures or artefacts carried by the army (for example, the ash and elm) as well as local timber supplies. Heather was also found in the ovens and may have indicated part of the roofing structure of the oven, or equally the use of turf as fuel. Remembering Caesar's comment about his troops constructing and thatching shelters over their tents during a winter campaign in Gaul, it is possible that turf could have been used as a thatch, but it seems unlikely that such structures could have been built at Kintore and escaped detection through the extensive excavations undertaken. Dung was also found and may have been used as a fuel in the ovens. The use of different fuels could indicate preferences in the way that different units cooked and fired their ovens, although the use of wood as a fuel was predominant.

There are excavated areas within the camp seemingly devoid of ovens. It is possible that these gaps represent genuine absence, rather than the later destruction of deposits, and that they could reflect areas of the camp zoned for activities other than tented settlement for troops (if it is reasonably assumed that the ovens were sited close to where the soldiers were housed), or that the housing of the men in this area left little archaeological trace. They could also reflect areas for storage, animals, or perhaps the position of the headquarters and officers' accommodation. At present no clear pattern can be discerned that would enable a model of the internal settlement of the camp to be ascertained, although the lack of clarity may also relate to different phases of occupation blurring the evidence.

The pits that have been excavated at Kintore also appear to be randomly scattered throughout the camp. While fewer are known than ovens, it is possible that some of the other undated pits recorded through the excavations may be Roman in date. Those that have been identified as Roman have not furnished the necessary environmental evidence suggesting their use as latrines, but the free-draining soils at Kintore may mean that any faecal parasites have not survived. Many of the pits contained general waste products, including food debris and general refuse, and some charred plant remains were found, which might indicate possible crop processing on site. This appears to have been a cleaned crop, with the grain becoming charred through drying or food processing. There was also an absence of grain from the ovens, suggesting that large-scale processing of whole grain was not being undertaken, and that that a meal or flour-based product was being cooked.

The majority of the ovens at Kintore are assumed to have been constructed for the purpose of baking bread. However, some of the ovens produced a small amount of material associated with metalworking, although some of the slag may have been re-deposited. Certainly the army would have had to make ongoing repairs and carry out routine maintenance on their equipment, particularly when located some distance from a permanent fort, so evidence for metalworking should not be wholly unexpected. Carbonised wooden bowls were also found, confirming that the army carried wooden vessels alongside metal and pottery on campaign. A few of the pits and ovens contained metal finds comprising tools, fittings and fastenings, nails, hobnails and other fragments. Many of these objects were iron bindings such as staples, fasteners, linch pins, and binding strips ripped off wooden objects, such as storage chests, with the wood presumably being salvaged for other purposes such as fuel. Other objects included the remnants of a metal scythe, potentially indicating the gathering of fodder for horses, also possibly indicated by the presence of a tethering peg.

The knowledge provided by excavations at Kintore hints at the kind of information and research questions that can be asked through further excavations at other camp sites. It is worth noting that hardly any internal features were visible on the air photographs of Kintore and the pits recorded there demonstrate little regularity. Excavations of crop-mark sites generally produce far more information than can be gleaned from the air photographic evidence alone, Kintore proving a case in point. Geophysical survey can also furnish additional data.

Aerial Evidence

A number of camps in Britain have revealed evidence for rows of pits from aerial photography and geophysical survey. At Dalginross in Perthshire (see above and Plate 14), two parallel lines of pits are visible in the northern part of the camp and a further line is visible to the south. Other pits are visible elsewhere in small groups, and these presumably represent clusters of activity, whether representing areas where troops were stationed or rubbish pits for other disposal activity, perhaps relating to the quartering of animals. But the lines of pits are fascinating. Adapting the measurements from Hyginus (see Chapters 4 and 5)[61], their lengths correspond approximately to the twenty tents of two Roman centuries camping alongside one another. Similar double lines of pits within the camps at Inchtuthil in Perthshire, a few of which were excavated, have been interpreted as potential streets between groups of tents (Figure 54; also see Chapter 5). These excavated pits contained a small amount of pottery and probable sheep-ribs, suggesting that they were rubbish pits[62]. As with Dalginross, the lines of pits in one area (the south-west) correspond to the approximate length of a line of tents for a cohort. The space between the lines of pits, 4.5–5.5 m, is insufficient space for tents (see comments that Hyginus makes about space provision for tent rows – Chapter 4), so street lines between tents seems plausible and would fit with the evidence for the presence of street lines elsewhere (such as at Ardoch, noted earlier).

At Moss Side in Cumbria, a large number of pits have been recorded around the edges of the camp and its annexe and in linear patterns within the camp. Although unexcavated, it is possible that those around the edges represent the remains of ovens whereas those further in the interior are rubbish pits, but the results of the excavations at Kintore caution against such bold attribution. The pits within the camp do appear to be aligned on the entrances, again also suggesting that these lines could represent internal streets.

At Glenlochar in Dumfries & Galloway, one of the camps close to the fort exhibits a large number of pits within its interior (Figure 55), although these exhibit less regularity than Moss Side, Inchtuthil and Dalginross. A clear perimeter line of pits has been recorded, with all these pits lying at least 6 m from the line of the ditch, thereby allowing sufficient

55. Aerial view of the pits inside one of the camps at Glenlochar in Dumfries & Galloway, taken from the south-west in 1984. © Crown Copyright: RCAHMS. SC1164051. Licensor www.rcahms.gov.uk

space for the rampart. A more modern road bisects the camp, possibly on the alignment of the original entrances through the camp, and because the interior is so seemingly full of pits, it seems likely that areas devoid of pits were genuinely used for activities which did not require the excavation of rubbish pits, latrines or ovens. Furthermore, a couple of circular doughnut-shaped ring-ditches of unknown function and date are also visible within this camp's perimeter.

Finally, recent geophysical survey at Dalswinton Bankfoot in Dumfriesshire has suggested that one of the camps here, which revealed limited information through aerial survey, also has a wealth of pit-like features within its interior (many of which may be ovens); a line of slightly larger pits along one side of its perimeter may also be the remains of ovens[63].

While modern, small-scale interventions in camp interiors frequently record no Roman features, a body of data is gradually being accumulated which indicates that the interiors of these sites are worthy of more detailed study and that further research through geophysical survey and excavation is required.

ANNEXES

On a handful of temporary camp sites in Britain, additional smaller attached enclosures or annexes have been recorded. The majority of these are known from a group of camps in Scotland which enclose 25 hectares (around 63 acres) in size and run from Stirling to Montrose (see Chapter 9; Figure 56). Three of the camps on the Antonine Wall and one of the camps on Hadrian's Wall also exhibit such features. One camp in Wales, Arosfa

Roman Camps in Britain

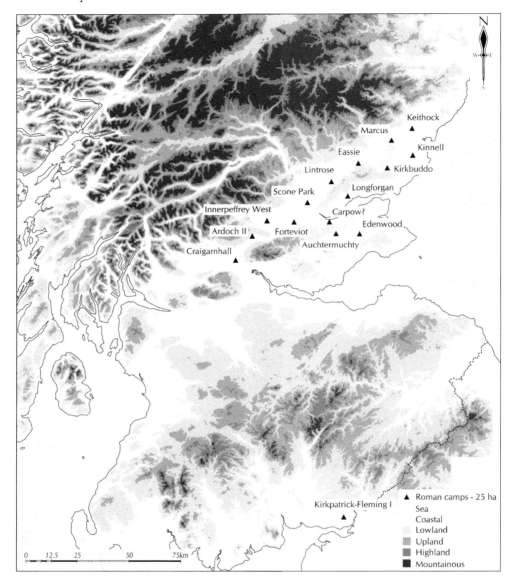

56. Distribution map of the 25-hectare (63-acre) camps in Scotland.

Garreg in Carmarthenshire, has a possible annexe on one end, although this earthwork is not widely accepted as Roman in date[64].

These annexes attached to the camps in the Scottish 25-hectare group are generally attached just outside the front of the camp, to the side of the main entrance, the *porta praetoria*. Although we do not know the function of these structures and there has been limited geophysical survey and excavation in these areas, having them outside the main gate is potentially significant as to their importance. Excavations in the annexe of the camp of Longforgan near Dundee, Angus, revealed a small circular scoop of uncertain date or

102

57. Aerial view of the annexe attached to the camp at Marcus in Angus, taken from the south in 1986. © Crown Copyright: RCAHMS. SC1164042. Licensor www.rcahms.gov.uk

function – analysis of the fill of the annexe ditch suggested it was backfilled quickly, but this could have been due either to deliberate back-filling or rapid weathering[65].

The majority of annexes attached to camps in this group display uniformity, enclosing between 1 and 1.3 hectares (2½ to just over 3 acres), with one exception at Longforgan, which encloses just over 1.5 hectares (3¾ acres). The camp at Marcus in Angus is one of the camps in this 25-hectare (63 acre) group and possesses a small annexe on its south-west side which encloses just over 1 ha (over 2½ acres) (Figure 57); here the entrances to the main camp are protected with *tituli* and the annexe possesses a *titulus* on one side. Entrances are sometimes, but not always, visible on annexes, and occasionally *tituli* have been recorded. All known annexes appear to use part of the main ditch of the camp to which they are attached as one side, although no excavation has taken place on the intersections between annexe and main camp to establish relative chronology. Indeed, none of the annexes attached to the 25-hectare camps has produced any dating evidence, and neither have the nearby camps. However, those along the Antonine Wall are presumed to be Antonine in date, particularly the camp at Little Kerse in Stirlingshire, where excavations of the annexe ditch produced pottery fragments of early Antonine date. The small camp at Moss Side in Cumbria on Hadrian's Wall may be Flavian to Hadrianic in date, although there is no dating evidence to confirm this suggestion[66].

However, the function of these structures is mysterious; because the relationship between these and their adjoining camps is unknown, it is possible that they could have functioned as some form of roadside post at a completely different time, or before the main force housed in the larger camp arrived, or housed troops after the departure of the main army. It is also possible that a detachment of troops might often have been left behind to guard a camp when the main body was temporarily absent, perhaps on campaigning duties elsewhere. During the Batavian revolt of AD 69 (in the area of the modern-day Netherlands), Tacitus informs us that the Roman commander Vocula left behind small groups of men to guard the command posts[67]. But the known details do suggest some options over others. For example, using a small annexe when the main body of the camp had been abandoned means that one side (that of the main camp) has an internal ditch and external rampart, which would mean that it was defensively weakened, although an additional rampart could have been constructed within the annexe area. It is equally possible that they were in operation at the same time as the occupation of the main camp.

It is intriguing, therefore, to speculate that small units may have been attached to the forces occupying the larger camps. Such units may have formed a crucial role in reconnaissance, such as scouts (*exploratores*) sent out in advance of the main force to assess suitable camp sites and gather intelligence, and may have set up camp some time prior to the arrival of the larger army, who then proceeded to camp alongside. But if they established camp before the main force started constructing its camp, then the question remains regarding the rampart and ditch of the adjoining side, unless it is just accepted that the perimeter at this point had two ramparts with a ditch in between. Standing units of *exploratores* may have existed from the second century AD[68], and the Vindolanda Tablets (see Chapter 4) report troops being stationed away from their main base[69].

Equally, these annexes could have housed hostages, camp followers or other groups of people or animals that were not deemed appropriate to house within the main body of the camp, possibly for reasons of noise, smell or general convenience. At one of the camps at Glenlochar in Dumfries & Galloway, the camp itself reveals evidence on air photographs of numerous pits in the interior (Figure 55), but there is a lack of such pits in the annexe. If the annexes housed hostages, settlement activity such as pits would be expected, and presumably such persons, as with most additional baggage, could be located anywhere. In addition, they would be more secure as prisoners if housed in the main body of the camp, where they would be under stronger guard than outside the perimeter. Some classical texts refer to camp followers (*lixae*) and, although these sometime appear to have been inside the camp, elsewhere they appear to have camped outside the rampart[70]. At the fort of Vindolanda, close to Hadrian's Wall in Northumberland, a series of circular stone huts have been excavated, similar to the stone roundhouses used in contemporary Iron Age settlements. Various theories for these buildings have been put forward, including that they housed

Iron Age workers or even refugees fleeing fighting between the Romans and the Iron Age communities living north of Hadrian's Wall, or that they imprisoned hostages taken during campaigns against the northern tribes[71]. Whether or not this seemingly unusual evidence from Vindolanda can be translated into similar activities outside temporary camps remains to be seen.

It is also possible that horses could have been housed in annexes, in which case one should expect to see these with more frequency than is currently known. And as cavalry barracks have now been identified in forts, it is apparent that horses were housed within the perimeter of these so there would not necessarily be a reason to exclude them from the main body of the camp when on campaign, although in the absence of permanent buildings in which to stable the horses one wonders just where they were located.

It seems likely that the annexes attached to the camps on Hadrian's Wall and the Antonine Wall would have been used for a different purpose than those attached to marching camps, if the assumption that these were construction camps is correct. For example, an army engaged in construction work on the mural barriers may have needed additional space to store tools and other supplies, although this should suggest that they would be ubiquitous along both frontiers, which is not the case. But these rare examples may have housed some sort of industrial activity. Until further work is undertaken on annexes, they remain enigmatic.

We are, therefore, presented with a wealth of archaeological evidence enabling us to interpret remains as belonging to the Roman army and to start to understand aspects of military dictat and the life of soldiers on the move. In many instances, the ways in which we can identify camps are through their perimeter defences – ramparts and ditches – constructed to provide a 'walled city'[72] within which rows upon rows of soldiers were housed inside leather tents with space provided for other activities. It is frequently the ditches, revealed through differential crop-markings from the air, which provide the first indicator of the presence of a temporary camp. Indeed, some 65 per cent of camps known in Britain are only recorded through crop-markings revealing buried ditches, and if some camps were only protected through the provision of ramparts then many more will have been lost to the plough in the intervening centuries. Given that so many are only known from the air, we are fortunate that they possessed distinctive features such as gates and were standardised shapes, enabling them to be recognised and interpreted as camps. Even the camps that were not the usual square or rectangular form that was so standardised and recognisable had distinctive rounded corners and may well have distinctive entrance protection in the form of *tituli* and *claviculae*. Annexes to camps have been recognised, but their purpose remains unknown. Finally, some camps have revealed additional features from the air and through excavations – in recent years we have gained knowledge of some internal structures within camps, particularly ovens used by the soldiers for baking bread and the pits that were probably used for latrines and other forms of waste disposal. In particular, extensive excavations at Kintore in Aberdeenshire have transformed our understanding of the use and occupation of camps and the daily life of soldiers briefly stationed at temporary outposts far away from the heart of Rome.

9

Distribution, Chronology and Context

DISTRIBUTION

The survival of camps, detailed in Chapter 7, dictates where we have been able to locate and identify them today. Figure 2 shows the distribution of camps across Britain. This distribution is biased by a number of factors. These include the areas in Britain where their survival is most likely – it is no surprise to see clusters in the upland zones, where chances of earthwork survival are greater. When it comes to more lowland areas, many are recorded along the routes of Roman roads and in the vicinity of Roman forts and fortresses. While there should again be no surprise here, this also reflects areas that have seen repeated flying by Roman aerial archaeologists including O. G. S. Crawford and Professor J. K. St Joseph (see Chapter 6)[1]. In recent years, expansion of aerial survey away from known Roman hubs and route ways has identified camps in more diverse locations.

Figure 2 also reveals a distinct lacuna in the south and east of Britain. There is no reason to suggest that these were not areas that saw active campaigning in the initial conquest phases of the AD 40s. Indeed, Caesar's two brief sojourns into southern England should also have left archaeological traces. There have been suggestions that his troops reached Wheathampstead near St Albans in Hertfordshire and also Gosbecks Farm near Colchester in Essex but neither as yet has been confirmed archaeologically. The movement of Claudius' invasion army has also been the subject of debate, with Richborough in Kent and Fishbourne near Chichester in Sussex presenting rival bids for the landing locations for the invasion forces. The dearth of camps in both counties contributes nothing to the debate. Indeed, literary sources and archaeological evidence suggests that the movement of Roman forces through parts of south-east England was fairly rapid. Nevertheless, there is no reason not to expect the troops to have constructed defensive perimeters at each overnight stop. In Chapters 3 and 8, we noted the possibility that troops may have used methods other than ramparts and ditches to demarcate the perimeter. If Germanicus, only a generation or two earlier, constructed camps with palisades around the perimeter[2], there is reason to suppose that this may have been the case in parts of southern Britain. Indeed, the distribution of camps in Britain could be used to argue that the construction of a perimeter ditch on a temporary camp was not standard practice in the early part of the Claudio-Neronian period (AD 41–68) but was by the time of the Flavian activities (AD 69–96). A number of camps are recorded from modern-day France (and also Germany) with some, like Alesia, attributed to the campaigns of Caesar in the mid-first century BC. Camps defended by perimeter ditches were deployed on the continent prior to the Flavian period, but rarely in the quantities recorded in Britain. However, we have already noted the advantage that Britain has due to our aerial pioneers having Roman interests and this could be as much to do with survey biases as actual archaeological evidence.

It is also possible that the gaps in our knowledge stem from differing practices by Roman forces at different times. Many of the counties of southern and eastern England are agriculturally rich and have produced a wealth of archaeological crop-markings, and we would hope that Roman temporary camps should be identified from aerial survey and photography. Only further archaeological evidence will be able to support or refute this suggestion.

When looking elsewhere in Britain, it is abundantly apparent that our knowledge is still extremely patchy. Agricultural practices, settlement development and industrial activity have all combined to leave us a partial record. Some of the early fort and fortress sites in Britain lie under modern-day towns, and occasional excavations may reveal segments of early ditches which may relate to temporary camp occupations.

Yet despite the gaps in south-eastern England, a number of camps are known in the south-west and in the northern part of east Anglia and into the Midlands. For example, a number of camps are now known in Devon, an area which saw significant military activity with the *legio II Augusta* pushing into the south-west in the early conquest phases (commanded by the later Emperor Vespasian [AD 69–79] – see Chapter 2). This resulted in the establishment of a fortress for the legion at Exeter in the late AD 50s. After the departure of the legion in the mid-70s AD, Exeter developed into a civilian town (*Isca Dumnoniorum*) but recent discoveries through aerial photography and excavation of new forts, fortlets and camps in the area point towards a considerable amount of military activity in the south-west in the first century AD.

In the Marches and into Wales, few patterns can be discerned as to the distribution of camps (also see below). It is possible that some of the apparent blanks may be due to early campaigns not constructing perimeter ditches, but here, as elsewhere in Britain, there are substantial areas of improved pasture. In these circumstances, the remains of camps may lie below the surface but have not yet been detected. Remote sensing techniques (see Chapter 6) could help to fill the gap, both in identifying new sites and enabling more detailed analyses of existing ones.

In the north of Britain, the propensity for camps to cluster along Roman roads and around existing fort sites is clear (Figure 2), and lines of march become more apparent. This will be discussed further below. But another interesting element in the distribution map is that a number of camps lie in coastal zones, particularly on the River Solway and in parts of eastern and western Scotland. These potentially indicate links between the forces travelling by land and those using sea routes. It is possible that these were points where the army and fleet met to share 'supplies and high spirits' and boast about their exploits[3]. Tacitus referred to the governor Agricola crossing with his fleet somewhere in south-west Scotland[4], but there is debate about what the translation of the Latin actually means and the passage could relate to either the use of the fleet or a land-based crossing of the Solway Firth or the River Annan. A land route into south-west Scotland from Carlisle is evident from the distribution of camps and the (undated) Roman road in this area. But use of the fleet was not confined to Agricola's activities in the first century AD. Along the south side of the Solway coast, a camp is recorded at Knockcross[5] at the western end of Hadrian's Wall. On the north side they are known at various points, including one either side of the mouth of the River Annan, at Hillside Annan and Annanfoot[6]. Further west, coastal camps are sited overlooking river mouths opening onto the Solway Firth, close to the Lochar Water and overlooking the entrance to the River Nith (Ward Law – Figure 49; see Chapter 8). Some of these camps could relate to sea-based operations and/or supply of the more permanent bases in Dumfries & Galloway. We might expect to find camps at the mouths of other rivers in this area, but more aerial survey in dry years coupled with ground-based fieldwork is required. There are one or two antiquarian accounts of camps along the coast here, but these either remain unconfirmed or have been disproved. The camp at Ward Law lies close to a fortlet (Lantonside) of suspected but unconfirmed second-century AD Antonine date. Although the date of Ward Law is also unknown, it is possible that the two sites performed similar functions at different times, potentially being involved in the oversight and distribution of supplies to garrisons lying further up the River Nith[7].

The Roman road in south-west Scotland appears to head towards Loch Ryan, but camps and forts along this road remain elusive (and the presumed fort close to Loch Ryan unlocated). Certainly, a site on the Rhins of Galloway would make a suitable departure point for any potential offensive across the Irish Sea. Tacitus does record that Agricola drew up his troops and contemplated an invasion of Ireland[8].

Also facing the North Channel and further up the coast lie two camps at Girvan Mains in Ayrshire. One of these produced a small fragment of late first-century AD glass from its ditch during excavations, reinforcing the idea of troops looking across to Ireland during the Agricolan campaigns. This site, close to where the Girvan Water meets the North Channel, is the first point on the west coast north of Loch Ryan where it would be feasible to site a camp and represents a good location for the meeting of land and sea forces on the west coast.

A few camps are recorded close to the sea on the east coast of Scotland[9]. Across the Tay from the fortress of Carpow (also see Chapter 5) lies such an example, a small camp called St Madoes in Perthshire. Because of a connection between Carpow and the campaigns of the Emperor Severus in the third century AD, it has been proposed that a bronze coin or medallion struck in AD 209 depicting a bridge of boats or pontoon with the word '*traiectus*' (crossing) on its reverse applies to a crossing of the Tay at this point[10]. The discovery of St Madoes has led to suggestions that this was a bridgehead camp.

On the north side of the Montrose Basin in Angus lies another small camp at Dun (Plate 19). A fragment of first-century AD Roman pottery found in small-scale excavations has been used to suggest that it functioned as a stores depot for Flavian operations up the east coast, when Tacitus records that Agricola pushed forward by land and sea in his sixth season, and infantry, cavalry and marines often met in the same camp[11]. Whether the camp was large enough to have functioned as a meeting place for such a force is questionable (it enclosed less than 3 hectares – around 7 acres), but certainly some link between land and sea campaigns seems a likely function because of its sheltered embankment at a shore-side location. Furthermore, it lies less than 10 km from the Flavian fort at Stracathro and would have represented a convenient point for bringing supplies to this and potentially some of the other forts in Strathmore in Angus.

If these coastal camps do represent stopping places for the fleet and the supply of the land-based troops, then more camps at suitable marine points should be expected. But the land campaigns in Britain rarely seem to have followed coastal routes, with the main exceptions being the north side of the Tay estuary and the Solway Firth. Elsewhere, forts are known in coastal locations, particularly at the ends of the two frontier Walls and again in the later Roman Empire in the south and east of Britain with the establishment of Saxon Shore forts. But these latter military establishments were to protect the province from external raiders rather than relating to its conquest and garrisoning.

With regard to the use of the fleet in the conquest of Britain, the archaeological evidence is lacking, but it seems likely that governors of Britain deployed the fleet in tactical support where necessary and, indeed, Agricola is credited with sending the fleet on a circumnavigation of the island[12]. It certainly seems likely that the Roman forces would have deployed the fleet in tactical support in areas where the terrain rendered the supply of land campaigns difficult. But our knowledge of sea campaigning is extremely limited and currently does little to help understand the chronologies and contexts for the temporary camps found throughout Britain.

CHRONOLOGY AND CONTEXT

There are essentially four ways in which it is possible to assign or propose dates for temporary camps. Firstly, the historical context enables us to allocate dates on the basis of probability given the geographic location of the camps. For example, in most of England and Wales, camps are assumed to belong to the first century AD because these were the periods of conquest in these areas. But closer dating than the first to fourth centuries AD is very difficult: Britain suffered periods of unrest at various times throughout the Roman occupation and camps may have been constructed by troops moving through conquered areas that were difficult to control, or because they were familiar with constructing perimeter defences on all occasions so continued to do so even if such a level of protection was not necessary, or they were on training or manoeuvres. Although most of the English and Welsh camps are assumed to be of first-century AD date because this was the main period of campaigning and conquest, it does not necessarily follow that all camps south of Hadrian's Wall were first constructed in the first century AD. North of Hadrian's Wall, camps are usually attributed to campaigns in the late first, mid-second and early third centuries AD, with most of those north of the Forth–Clyde isthmus generally allocated to the Flavian campaigns in the first century AD or those of Severus and his sons in the early third century AD, because these are the two main recorded incursions into this area. There are tantalising clues in the literature to other campaigns in northern Britain (see Chapter 2), but, as yet, there has been limited work to try and gain any tangible evidence for these and our archaeological knowledge is frustratingly barren. The second way to assign the occupation of a camp to a particular period or date is on the basis of association, perhaps because it is located outside a fort with more secure

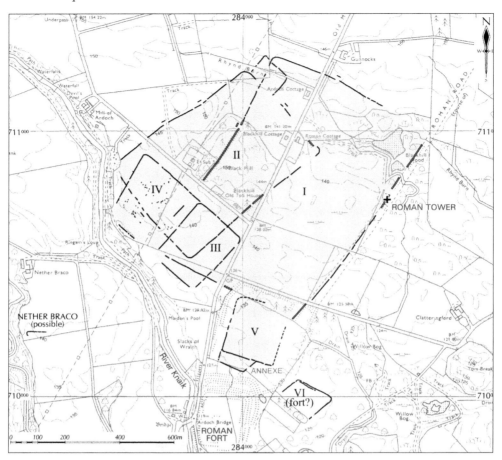

58. Plan of the camps at the fort of Ardoch in Perthshire.

archaeological dates for its foundation and abandonment, or because it has a relationship with a Roman road. The third is through ground survey and excavation, which can help to determine the relative sequence in which camps (and other sites) were constructed. Fourthly and finally, radiocarbon dating programmes and stratified artefacts from excavations may supply an indication of absolute date. But a combination of a lack of systematic excavation and a paucity of datable artefacts from secure archaeological contexts means that the date of the occupation of the majority of camps in Britain can only be assumed or guessed. Furthermore, the evidence is blurred when the same camp site is re-occupied more than once, whether on the exact same geographic footprint or in an overlapping sequence. As camps were enclosures occupied for a relatively short space of time it is unsurprising that we struggle to pin down their occupation dates, and with the exception of the very few sites that have provided good archaeological dating evidence, most of our presumptions are based on evidence and theories that are tenuous. However, this does not prevent us from using such evidence and theories; it is just that we must accept the fragile nature of our assumptions and hope that further work will help to flesh out the picture.

One of the sites which fits within two of the less secure dating categories noted above is that at Ardoch in Perthshire. The fort at Ardoch survives as a very impressive earthwork, and is one of the best-preserved earthen forts in Britain (Plate 20). Excavations in the 1890s and more recently have identified that the fort was occupied during both the Flavian (late first century AD) and Antonine (mid-second century AD) conquests of the area, which helps explain the complexity of the visible remains – the ramparts and ditches around its perimeter. On the plain to the north of the fort cluster a group of at least five camps which intersect one another (Figure 58); three have stretches of rampart and ditch still surviving as upstanding earthworks. The camps range in size from 4.3 ha (just under 11 acres) to 52 ha (129 acres). Excavations on the camps have been limited and focused at points where different ditches intersect one another. Even though no dating evidence has been recovered from these excavations, they have enabled a level of understanding of the sequence of construction of these structures. The smallest camp (camp V on Figure 58) lies within the annexe to the fort (often termed the '*procestrium*') and survives as a very low earthwork. Although the relationship between this camp and the annexe is unknown, it seems possible that the camp pre-dated the annexe because excavations revealed that the ditch of the camp had been deliberately filled in. Although the date of construction of the annexe is also not known, it accompanied either the first- or second-century AD occupations of the fort.

To the west of the fort and annexe, camps III and IV are known from crop-markings on air photographs (Figure 59). Excavations in 1969 on the smaller, eastern camp III suggested that the ditch had been deliberately filled in. Tiny fragments of Roman coarse ware and mortaria were recovered from these excavations, but were not large enough to provide a suggestion of date. Professor St Joseph, who conducted these excavations, interpreted the in-filling of the ditch as taking place due to the enlargement of the camp into camp IV, but this is not the only possible explanation for deliberate re-filling of the ditches, which could have happened subsequently. It is also possible that camp IV was the earlier of the two, and was later reduced in size (and therefore became camp III).

Excavations of the ditch intersections revealed that camp III was earlier than camp II which was, in turn, earlier than camp I. Short stretches of the rampart of camp II were slighted at the location of street lines for camp I, as noted in Chapter 8. Indeed, camp I, the largest camp, appears to be the latest Roman construction at Ardoch, overlying both the undated annexe to the fort and the Roman road and watch-tower to the east (both of which are assumed to be first-century AD in date, or second-century AD at the latest). Using historical sources, it has therefore been suggested that this large camp dated to the Severan campaigns of the early third century AD, and no evidence has yet come to light to refute this proposal.

This camp is one of a series of camps of this size (around 54 hectares/130 acres) known in a line running from Stirlingshire through Perthshire and Angus to southern Aberdeenshire (Figure 60). Although not a consistent distance from one another, the distances between these camps (of between 10 and 25 km/7–17 Roman miles) could represent a good day's march by a campaigning army. The Roman author Vegetius refers to the army training by marching some 20 Roman miles (30 km) on manoeuvres and up to 24 miles (35 km) at a faster pace[13] so these distances are well within the capabilities of Roman forces on the move.

59. Aerial view of parts of camps I, II, III and IV at Ardoch in Perthshire, taken from the north-west in 1986. © Crown Copyright: RCAHMS. SC355878. Licensor www.rcahms.gov.uk

All the camps are broadly rectangular in shape and appear to have had six gates (one at each end and two in either side), which were protected by *tituli* (see Chapter 8).

No dating evidence has been recovered from any of the camps in this apparent sequence (except a stray early second-century AD Trajanic coin from Grassy Walls in Perthshire, but this was found in the vicinity in 1907 and does not provide any security of date). If these camps do represent the campaigns of the Emperor Septimius Severus, then the historian Cassius Dio informs us that the soldiers campaigned to the 'furthest point of the island'[14]. Although the easternmost camp of this group, Kair House, lies close to where the edge of the Highlands approaches the sea, it is hardly the tip of Scotland. But it could have been north of the lands occupied by the Caledonian tribes and Cassius Dio could be referring to the area beyond the Caledonians rather than to the northern extremities of Scotland; he also commented that the Severan campaigns 'passed through' Caledonia. Although entirely

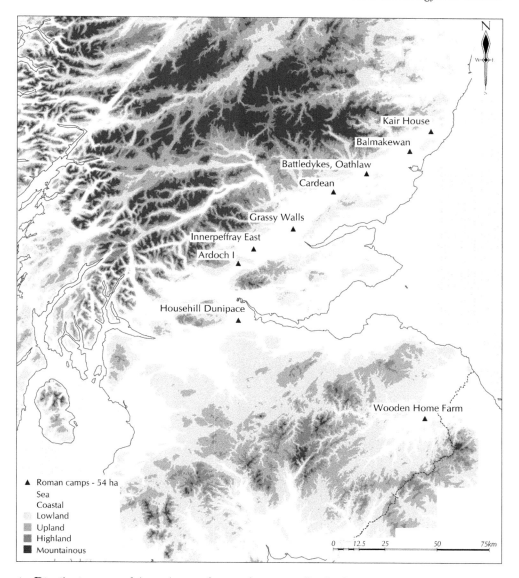

Kair House ▲

Balmakewan ▲

Battledykes, Oathlaw ▲

Cardean ▲

Grassy Walls ▲

Innerpeffray East ▲

Ardoch I ▲

Househill Dunipace ▲

Wooden Home Farm ▲

▲ Roman camps - 54 ha
   Sea
   Coastal
   Lowland
   Upland
   Highland
   Mountainous

0   12.5   25   50   75km

60. Distribution map of the 54-hectare (130-acre) camps in Scotland.

based on supposition, the suggestion that these extremely large camps could have held troops engaged in campaigns in the early third century AD is appealing.

Returning to the camps at Ardoch, the dating of the other camps remains unknown. However, camp II, enclosing almost 27 hectares (66 acres), also fits with a sequence of camps with a similar distribution to those enclosing 54 hectares (130 acres) (Figures 56 and 60). These camps, enclosing some 25 hectares (63 acres), run from Stirlingshire through Perthshire and Angus in two lines (or an elliptical arrangement). Several lie adjacent to, or intersecting with, 54-hectare camps, but the relationship has only been tested at Ardoch. As with their larger

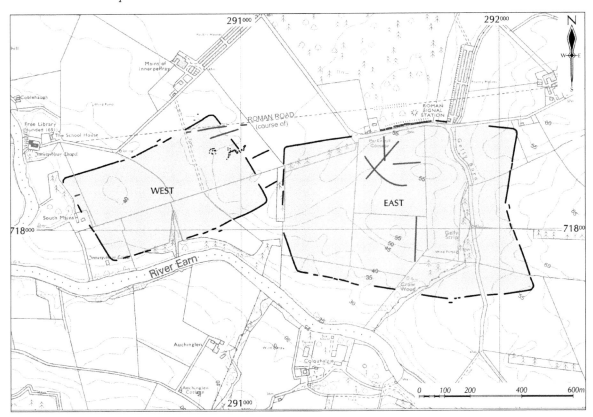

61. Plan of the two camps at Innerpeffray in Perthshire.

neighbours, these camps are broadly rectangular in shape and appear to have had six gates (one at each end and two in either side) which were protected by *tituli*. In addition, quite a few of these had attached camps or annexes (see Chapter 8), enclosing around one additional hectare (2.5 acres). There is more consistency in the spacing between these camps, averaging 11–15 km (7–10 Roman miles), again well within the capabilities of the Roman army.

On the assumption that these camps form a series occupied by the same army, which seems likely given their uniformity and regular spacing, it is not possible to determine whether they represent a route out and back or whether the army re-occupied the same camps on their return. Relatively small-scale trenching has taken place at a number of the camps in this group, but at no point has an obvious re-cut of the ditch been observed. This does not mean that the camps were not re-occupied, but that any re-occupation did not require large-scale re-cutting of the perimeter ditch. Furthermore, we equally do not know whether the soldiers occupying these camps were campaigning against the local population which occupied Strathmore and the Carse of Gowrie, or were traversing en route to tribes which occupied land further north. It is also possible that they represent the movement of two armies of equal size, but again this is almost impossible to prove archaeologically. Although not all the camps in this group have annexes, both apparent lines of march

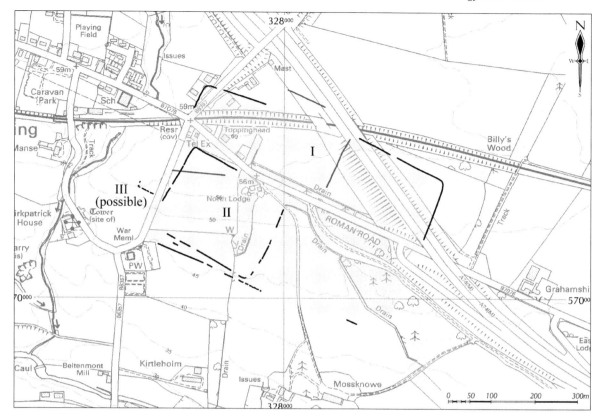

62. Plan of Kirkpatrick-Fleming in Dumfriesshire.

possess camps with annexes, so they cannot be separated through the interpretation of these additional enclosures.

No dating evidence has been recovered from any of the camps in this series. Their potential date has hitherto hinged on their relationship with and similarities to those of *c.* 54 ha (130 acres) in size, also not dated. Certainly both groups share a morphological likeness (both comprise rectangular camps with six gates protected by *tituli*) and also follow a similar line of march through Strathmore (Stirlingshire, Perthshire and Angus). However, this geographical relationship could be due to the use of maps and itineraries rather than temporal proximity, and our only knowledge of sequence between them is from Ardoch, where the 26-ha camp was earlier than its larger counterpart, but neither series has provided any absolute evidence for date. At nearby Innerpeffray (Figure 61), across the river from the Roman fort of Strageath, recent excavations[15] have taken place on the intersection between the 25-ha camp and the Roman road in this area. These recorded that the road was later, although this road need not have been of Roman origin (it could, for example, represent the route of the medieval road in the area). But its route does line up with the known stretches of Roman road in this area. The Roman road is conventionally assumed to be Flavian (first century AD) in date, due to its association with the watch-towers along its route which have produced fragmentary dating evidence, but the dating of the road is unproven and an Antonine (second century AD) date is also not implausible. If we can assume that the road is Roman in date, this suggests that this camp and the others in the 25-hectare series would date to the early Antonine period at the latest. Although the annexe of the smaller 25-ha camp appears to intersect the perimeter of the larger (54-ha camp), the relationship between the two has not been tested by excavation.

Furthermore, in southern Scotland, at Kirkpatrick-Fleming in Dumfriesshire, lies another camp of 25 hectares in size with a possible annexe to one side (Figure 62). Pottery recovered during excavations of the ditch of this potential annexe suggested dates ranging from AD 100–150, therefore probably of Hadrianic or possibly Antonine occupation, but there was no clear link between this annexe-type feature and the camp and, therefore, the dating of the pottery in its ditch cannot be extended to the dating of its 25-ha neighbour. However, if this additional ditch does represent a feature contemporary with the occupation of the main camp, possibly even housing a detachment of troops who arrived to join the main force after the construction and layout of the camp or arrived on site before the main army, then this could have implications for the dating of the 25-ha group as a whole. Furthermore, although of similar dimensions, the 25-hectare camp is too significantly geographically removed from the others in the series to be regarded as contemporary (Figure 56), unless an entire series of camps between the English border and the Forth–Clyde isthmus still awaits identification. This is unlikely but not impossible; it is more likely that it relates to adherence to the same rules of camp construction rather than the same force.

Other series of camps are recorded in Britain, but the vast majority of these lie north of the Forth–Clyde isthmus. In north-eastern Scotland, running through Aberdeenshire and Moray, lies a small group of four camps of similar dimensions to one another. All four are rectangular in form, appear to have six entrances protected by *tituli*, enclose some 44 hectares (110 acres) in size, and are sited, on average, some 20 km (13 Roman miles) apart. Two other camps have been grouped with this four (as depicted on Figure 63), but one (Raedykes) is significantly smaller (enclosing 39 ha/96 acres; see Chapter 8 and Figure 43) and the other (Logie Durno) is the largest known camp in northern Scotland (enclosing almost 57 ha/144 acres; also see Chapter 4 and Figure 22). The extensively excavated camp at Kintore (see Chapter 8) is a member of this group and the results of these excavations can help with our understanding of their construction and occupation. A combination of artefacts and radiocarbon dates suggests that the camp was primarily occupied in the Flavian period (first century AD), but that there may have been a secondary occupation in the late second/early third centuries AD. This strengthens the likelihood of a Flavian date for these 44-ha camps, with later potential re-occupation allowing for possible Severan (early third century AD) usage, although large-scale trenching of the perimeter ditch revealed no evidence for any re-cutting. It is, of course, possible that any refurbishment of the perimeter resulted in a larger ditch, which obliterated all traces of its predecessor. When first recorded and discussed by Professor St Joseph in the late 1950s, he initially grouped the 44-hectare (110-acre) and 54-hectare (130-acre) camps into a single series of around 49 hectares (120 acres). This was later refined in the early 1970s due to further aerial evidence becoming available, but also due to problems in making the camps fit with suggested chronologies[16]. This again highlights the dangers that we face when grouping camps together and making assumptions about their chronological contexts.

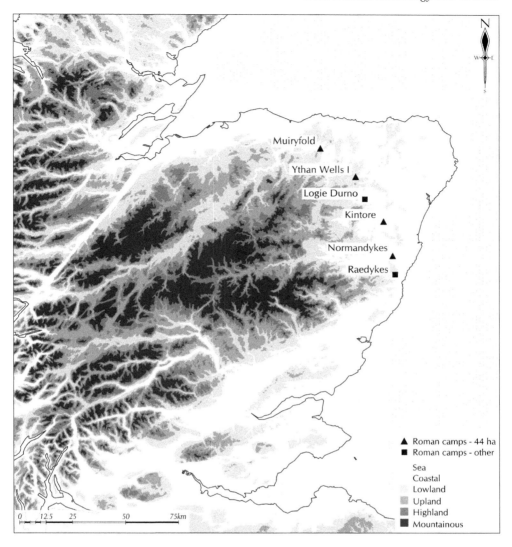

63. Distribution map of the 44-hectare (110-acre) camps and other large camps in north-eastern Scotland.

The camp at Logie Durno remains an anomaly (Figure 22). Although sited roughly midway between the camps of Kintore and Ythan Wells I, the overall distance between these two 44-hectare camps (25 km/17 Roman miles) is not excessive, as noted earlier. The size of the army which occupied this camp and, indeed, the smaller 44-ha (110-acre) camps, would have been extremely large and a marching column could have stretched for almost the distance between two camps (see Chapter 5).

South of the Forth–Clyde isthmus, the largest camps known anywhere in Britain and among the largest in the Roman Empire, lie alongside the Roman road of Dere Street in the Scottish Borders and Midlothian. Two of these, St Leonards (see Chapter 5; Figure

23) and Newstead V, enclose 70 ha (173 acres) and 67 ha (166 acres) respectively, and lie 11.5 km apart (just under 8 Roman miles). The same distance again to the north is the further extremely large camp of Channelkirk (Figure 45). Although the perimeter of this camp is only partially known, it is likely from the available dimensions that it enclosed a similar area. A similar distance again to the north is a further large camp (Pathhead III), of which only parts of two sides are known but, again, it seems plausible from the known lengths of side that it belonged to the same group as the three to the south.

No dating evidence has been recorded from any of these camps, but that at Newstead has been subject to a small amount of recent excavation[17]. Newstead is one of the pivotal sites north of Hadrian's Wall, where a Roman fort, lying on the south bank of the Tweed in the lee of the three peaks of the Eildon Hills (from where it gets its Latin name, *Trimontium*), is surrounded by a large cluster of annexes and temporary camps (Figure 64 and Plate 21). The fort itself was occupied during the conquests of both the first and second centuries AD; its final date of abandonment in the second century AD is unclear, but probably lay between AD 158 and around 180, with possible brief re-occupation during the Severan campaigns in the early third century AD. The latest coin recorded in the early twentieth-century excavations is of AD 177, but a stray find of a Caracallan intaglio (emperor from AD 209–217) has been recovered more recently.

The extremely large camp, of some 67 hectares (166 acres), at Newstead lies to the south of the fort but intersects its southern annexes. The camp itself has revealed two entrances with *tituli* in its two longer sides, suggesting that it probably had six gates in total (Figures 64 and 65). Excavations by Bradford University identified sizeable ditches which may have been later re-used for drainage purposes. Although undated, the fact that this camp avoids intersecting with the Roman fort could suggest that it is later in date than the occupation of the fort and therefore could be one of the later camps in the complex at Newstead[18].

Using historical sources to provide a context for a chain of such large camps, the most likely period is the Severan re-conquest of Scotland, where the presence of the Emperor Septimius Severus and his sons in AD 208–11 could account for their exceptional size, given the entourage and substantial baggage train that would have travelled with the Imperial party. Although using only historical sources that have not been corroborated archaeologically purely provides theoretical proposals, this is currently the best hypothesis that we have for these camps. The emperor would have continued his daily business of running the Roman Empire while on the march, the administration of which massively increases the numbers travelling with the army. Furthermore, the early third century AD does seem to be the period when the size of the garrison in northern Britain was at its greatest[19], and the line up Dere Street marks an obvious route for Severan armies to the Severan coastal fort at Cramond, near Edinburgh.

Little work has taken place on camp intersections south of the Forth–Clyde isthmus, despite excavations and small-scale trenches on individual camps. However, excavation work did take place at Chew Green in Northumberland in the 1930s (Figure 66), and detailed topographic survey more recently, of one of the few sites in Britain where the intersecting camps survive in earthwork form[20]. Although, again, undated, the earliest Roman structure at this site, high in the Cheviot hills, was a square camp with entrances protected by

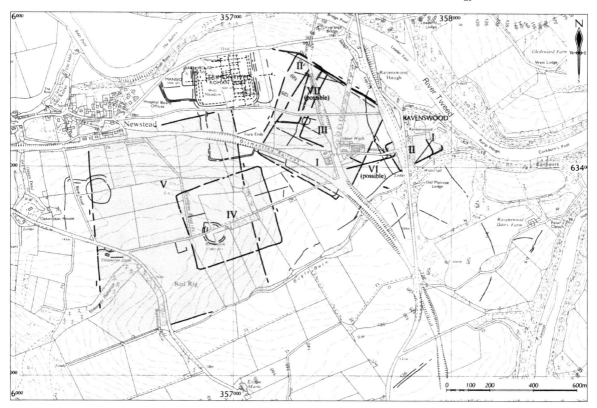

Above: 64. Plan of the fort and camps at Newstead in the Scottish Borders.

Right: 65. Aerial view of the east side of the very large (67 ha/166 acre) camp at Newstead in the Scottish Borders (and the eastern part of a neighbouring camp). Taken from the south-east in 1977. © Crown Copyright: RCAHMS. SC1164039. Licensor www.rcahms. gov.uk

claviculae (see Chapter 8). Unless the remains survive as earthworks, it is usually difficult to determine chronological relationships between camps without excavation. The most extreme example of an upstanding site with overlapping perimeters remains Y Pigwn in Brecknockshire (see Chapter 7 and Figure 36).

Elsewhere in Britain, it is difficult to identify many meaningful patterns in camp distributions and assign neighbouring camps to groups which may represent the sequential march of a campaigning force. Other groupings of two or three camps can be identified both north and south of the Forth–Clyde isthmus, but nothing on the scale of the 'series' of marching camps in the northern part of Scotland[21]. A pair of seemingly very similar camps is known from southern Perthshire, at Dunning and Carey (see Chapter 5; Figure 24). Both are rhomboid in shape, lie 15 km apart, and enclose 47.3 and 44.6 hectares (117 and 110 acres) respectively. But excavations of the two revealed a fragment of first-century AD pottery from Carey and second-century AD (Antonine) pottery from Dunning. Although this evidence, on the surface, suggests that the two are not contemporary, that from Dunning was from the fill of a *titulus* ditch, and that camp provided evidence for re-use, so the second-century AD date may not indicate its initial period of construction and use. This does highlight the limitations of assigning dates and periods to camps, even when dating evidence is recovered.

In northern England, it is again difficult to identify and group more than occasional pairs of camps. But along the Roman road running through the Stainmore pass (the modern A66), three camps are known which are of similar shape and size, enclosing 8–9.5 hectares (20–23 acres), and, more unusually, exhibit multiple gateways. At Rey Cross in County Durham, nine of a possible eleven entrances are known (see Chapter 5; Figure 20). Some 27 km to the north-west in Cumbria lies a camp at Crackenthorpe where some ten entrances have been identified. A further 22 km north-west lies a more irregular camp at Plumpton Head, where at least seven gates are known from three sides, its unusual shape being attributed to the need to avoid an area of boggy ground[22]. More recently, some 10 km east of Rey Cross, a further camp of similar size (8.3 ha/20.5 acres) has been identified at Cow Close, but not enough is known of its gateways to determine whether it should join the existing trio[23]. The Roman road across Stainmore runs through the camp at Rey Cross and changed alignment at the camp, suggesting that the road was the later of the two (although the camp has also revealed evidence for later re-use, with some of the gates showing signs of having been later blocked, and late third- or early fourth-century AD pottery found in the ditch and interior of the camp). The Roman road heads towards the fort at Carlisle, the foundation of which has been dated to AD 72/3 through analysis of its timbers[24]. This identifies the fort with the governor Petillius Cerealis (AD 71–73/4), and it has been suggested that the camps date to early penetration of this area[25], potentially under Cerealis (or possibly his predecessor, Vettius Bolanus, see Chapter 5). Although there is no secure dating evidence to support this proposal, it makes an interesting story and could relate to the origin of these camps, even if some were reused on potentially more than one occasion, and reused as late as the late third/early fourth century AD.

In the Marches and into Wales, tentative links have been made between camps in search of marching sequences, but only one of possibly three or four camps can be proposed with

66. Aerial view of Chew Green in Northumberland. © Crown Copyright: English Heritage

any confidence[26], and even this lacks the clarity of the Scottish series. This group starts with possibly Uffington and/or Whittington in Shropshire and then includes Pen Plaenau and Penrhos in Denbighshire[27]. Three of the four are only known through crop-markings (e.g. Figure 67 – Penrhos) but the fourth, Pen Plaenau, is an upstanding earthwork of which the majority of its perimeter rampart and ditch is visible, together with three entrances protected by curving internal *clavicula* ramparts (Figure 68). If the three or four camps were part of the same movement of troops, it seems likely that the others also possessed internal *claviculae* at their gates, but these have been lost to the plough and only simple entrance gaps are now known.

We have already noted that *tituli* are the most common form of gate type in use in Britain (Chapter 8). When it comes to dating camps through their entrance protection, camps with *tituli* are recorded from the second century BC, at the siege works near Numantia in Spain, to the later part of the Roman Empire. In contrast, the use of *claviculae* at entrances appears to have been popular over a much briefer timescale. One of the earliest proposed dates for a camp with *claviculae* is that at Mauchamp in France, attributed to the campaigns of Julius Caesar in 57 BC. Whether this does date to Caesar's campaigns is unproven, but

67. Aerial view of part of the north-west and north-east sides of the camp of Penrhos in Denbighshire, taken from the north in 2003. © Crown Copyright: Royal Commission on the Ancient and Historical Monuments of Wales. 2003-5089-47.

68. Aerial view of the camp of Pen Plaenau in Denbighshire, taken from the north in 2003. © Crown Copyright: Royal Commission on the Ancient and Historical Monuments of Wales. 2003-5124-64.

one of Caesar's siege camps at Alesia (52 BC) possessed an internal *clavicula* gate, thereby supporting their use in the mid-first century BC[28]. Furthermore, there are traces of *claviculae* at some of the camps in Spain and Egypt, again suggesting a Republican-period date[29]. Among the most securely dated camps with *claviculae* in the Roman Empire are those at Masada in Israel (Figure 1), dating to the siege of the fortress in AD 72–3[30]. The latest dates currently proposed for camps with *claviculae* are two at Nahal Hever in Israel (with external *claviculae*), dated to the Bar-Kokhba War of *c.* AD 132–5 (the time of the Emperor Hadrian), although the possibility that these could date to the Jewish War of the AD 70s has also been observed[31]. It is interesting to record that the then-governor of Britain, Julius Severus (*c.* AD 131–3), was sent to Judaea to deal with the Bar-Kokhba revolt[32]. Whether the presence of *claviculae* at these camps had anything to do with his arrival is unknown, but translated into a British context, the use of *claviculae* is generally attributed to the first century AD and the earlier part of the second century AD[33].

This dating is reinforced through other evidence; the classical author Hyginus, writing in this period (see Chapter 4), includes remarks on the use of both *tituli* and *claviculae* to protect the camp entrances[34], and *claviculae* are shown on the Column of Trajan in the Imperial Forum in Rome (Plate 7 and Figure 13). Depicting the story of Trajan's wars against the Dacians (AD 102–3 and AD 105–6), the frieze on the column incorporates depictions of the Roman army building camps. It is possible that *tituli* were not shown (although they are recorded on camps in Dacia – modern-day Romania) either because they were too difficult to portray graphically or because of sculptors' ignorance of Roman military life, but as *claviculae* are depicted they must have had some Roman manual or knowledge of defensive gate structures.

With regard to archaeological evidence, the distribution of camps with *claviculae* in Britain (Figure 69) and their proximity to dated first-century AD sites such as forts reinforces the suggestion that these were a first- and early second-century AD phenomenon. Certainly, their distribution is in areas where it is believed that armies were campaigning in the first century AD. Further clues are provided by the practice camps which proliferate in Wales. These camps are largely located outside auxiliary forts, and it is possible that auxiliaries and new recruits were being trained in the craft of building Roman structures, because these practice camps demonstrate evidence for the concentration on particular elements, including entrance features, rather than occupation[35]. By association, therefore, date ranges can be advocated for the practice camps in their vicinity, including those with *claviculae* gateways, on the basis of the known dates for the 'parent' forts. The majority of these forts were founded in the early Flavian period and are believed to have been abandoned by the AD 130s at the latest[36]. The lack of practice camps elsewhere in Britain, with the exception of a few possible examples on Hadrian's Wall[37], suggests that they were not commonplace throughout the Roman occupation but were the product of a specific phase of activity, possibly the training of new recruits.

The camp at Cawthorn in North Yorkshire has already been mentioned (Plate 13), sitting alongside two forts, one with an annexe. Both the camp and one of the forts and its annexe exhibit *claviculae* (probable 'cuspate' gates on the fort and annexe), and the whole complex has been dated to the period between AD 80 and the AD 120s, and only possibly slightly later[38].

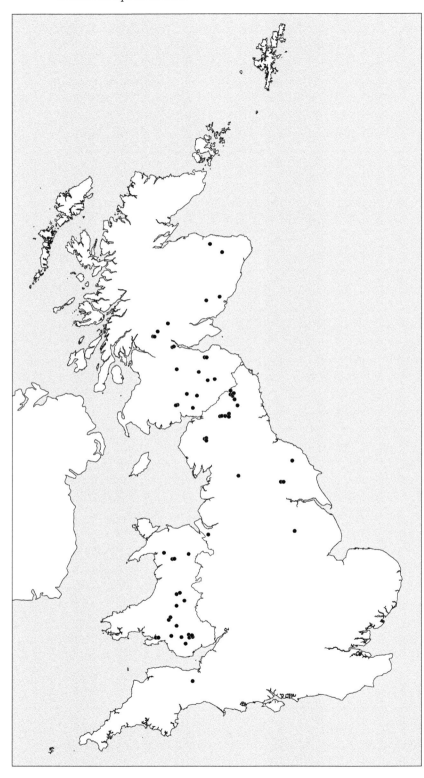

69. Map of camps
with *claviculae*
in Britain. ©
Crown Copyright:
RCAHMS. Licensor
www.rcahms.gov.uk

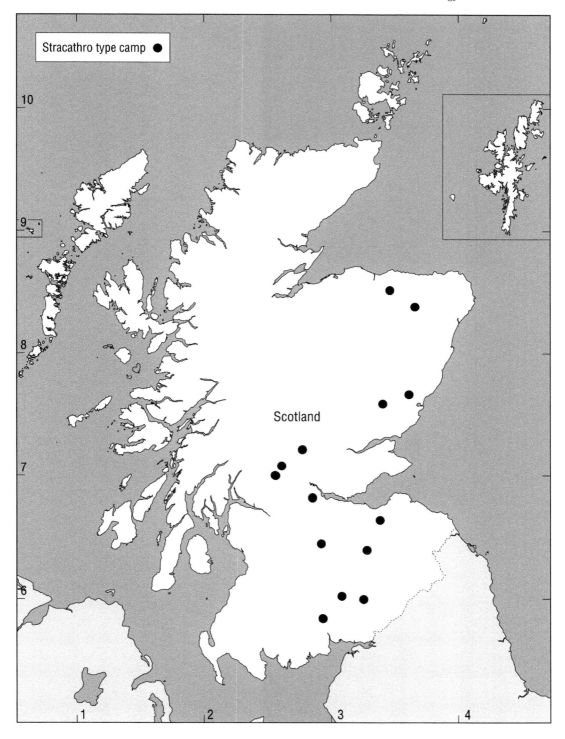

70. Map of camps with 'Stracathro-type' gates in Scotland. © Crown Copyright: RCAHMS. SC1124716. Licensor www.rcahms.gov.uk

71. Aerial view of the camp and fort (and its annexe) at Stracathro in Angus, taken from the south-west in 1982. © Crown Copyright: RCAHMS. SC355256. Licensor www.rcahms.gov.uk

Camps with *claviculae* gates in the form of the 'Stracathro-type' provide further indications of a first-century AD date, although none are securely dated. Due to their geographic locations (Figure 70), with two of the five most northerly camps exhibiting this gate design, some scholars have attempted to assign these to the campaigns of the first-century AD governor Agricola[39] (see Chapters 3 and 5), but the evidence cannot support such a specific attribution. However, on the basis of location, with some sited next to Flavian forts and others representing the earliest sites in a gathering ground (for example, Beattock Bankend, see below), a first-century AD (Flavian) date does seem the most likely date. One of the key sites here is Stracathro itself, where the perimeter of the camp intersects the annexe of the Flavian fort and is likely to be the earlier of the two (Figure 71).

As can be seen from Figure 70, the camps have a dispersed geography and also ranged in size (enclosing from 1.5 hectares to 24.5 hectares). It is possible that their rarity and seemingly irregular distribution could be due to a handful of officers – possibly a senior tribune or a camp prefect (*praefectus castrorum*) – posted in northern Britain with a specific legion for a limited period of time. If the gate form can be credited to a small number of officers from a particular legion, then perhaps the variability in size and shape also indicates significant flexibility in garrison sizes, and that troops frequently moved around in different size groupings, and divided and re-gathered together, depending on the demands of the terrain and reasons for particular manoeuvres. Tacitus informs us that Agricola split his force into three battle groups in his sixth season[40]; he was not stating this because it was an unusual event, but due to the subsequent attack on the ninth legion. The army was probably regularly divided for campaigns and manoeuvres, and the evidence for this may be one of the legacies of the archaeological remains of the 'Stracathro-type' camps. Another legacy is what can be inferred from their distribution regarding the responsible officers for camp layout and choice of entrance form. It has already been noted (Chapter 5) that Tacitus referred to Agricola choosing the camp sites himself[41], even though it seems more likely that this was a job for the camp prefect (*praefectus castrorum*). If Agricola had come up with such an innovative form of entrance protection for camps as the 'Stracathro-type' gates, it is likely that there would be some reference to this in his biography. These entrances may be the predilection of a particular *praefectus castrorum* in the *legio II Adiutrix*, a legion that was based in Britain for a short period of time (*c.* AD 71–86). However, the legion was stationed in Lincoln and Chester as well as campaigning in Scotland, and camps with these gateways are not currently recorded in England (although sites with external *claviculae* are known). But it is possible that the *praefectus castrorum* was only in post with that legion in Scotland for a limited period of time. The lack of Stracathro camps in England may be due to the difference between the permanent stationing of the legion further south and active campaigning duties and the construction of marching camps in Scotland. However, the attribution of these camps to a single legion is speculative and the only way to provide corroborating evidence for the *legio II Adiutrix* as the builders would be if camps with this distinctive gate form were identified in the modern-day countries of Romania, Hungary, Serbia and other areas where the legion was posted on its departure from Britain. The theory is interesting but unproven. It is equally possible that the gate form was developed by the officers of another legion, such as the *legio IX Hispana* whom Roy suggested were attacked by the Caledonian tribes at the Stracathro camp at Dalginross[42] – in this instance we should be looking to the Netherlands for more Stracathro-type camps, where this legion was posted after leaving Britain.

These ideas are purely speculative, but had Agricola or whoever was governor when these camps were built taken a detailed interest in camp construction, we should expect such techniques to be more widespread. An anonymous *praefectus castrorum* seems the most likely candidate, and one wonders where he was posted to after his time in Scotland, and why they are not more common in Scotland and further afield.

The Stracathro camps are just a group within the wider range of *claviculae*, but the narrowing of their likely date range to the later part of the first century AD (Flavian period) demonstrates that *claviculae* were in operation in Britain at this time. The two possibly Hadrianic camps at Nahal Hever in Israel[43] combine to suggest that some British examples could date to as late as the reign of the Emperor Hadrian (AD 117–138).

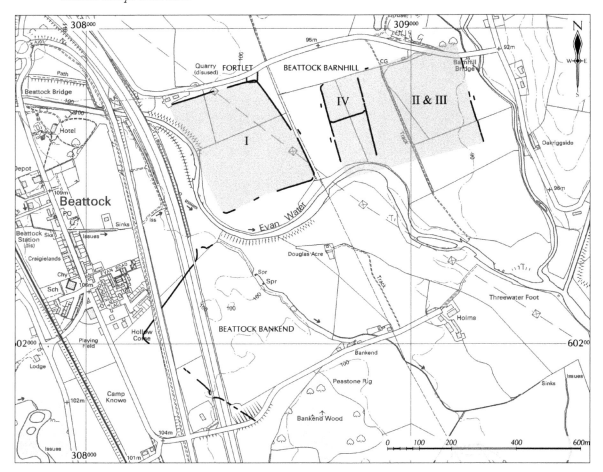

72. Plan of the camps at Beattock in Dumfriesshire.

In Dumfriesshire, a cluster of camps have been recorded as crop-markings from the air at Beattock, some 1 km north of the fort at Milton, on a plain on either side of the Evan Water in Annandale (Figure 72). That at Beattock Bankend, on the south side of the Water, possessed Stracathro-type gates, and was therefore probably constructed in the first century AD. On the north side of the water lies another camp which overlies a fortlet of probable first-century AD date (although this dating has not been confirmed, despite trial trenching in the 1980s). Adjacent to this camp is a further camp which exhibits potentially three different phases of use. A study of the alluvial history of the gravel deposits and palaeochannels of the Evan Water here concluded that at least one of the camps on the north side of the river (at Beattock Barnhill) was constructed across gravel deposits and palaeochannels that could only have formed after construction of the camp on the south side (Beattock Bankend)[44]. One of the camps at Beattock Barnhill is of a similar size and shape (enclosing just over 15 hectares/38 acres, with entrances protected by *tituli*) to a camp at Torwood, some 21 km to the south. About 21 km to the north of Beattock lies a cluster of camps around a fort

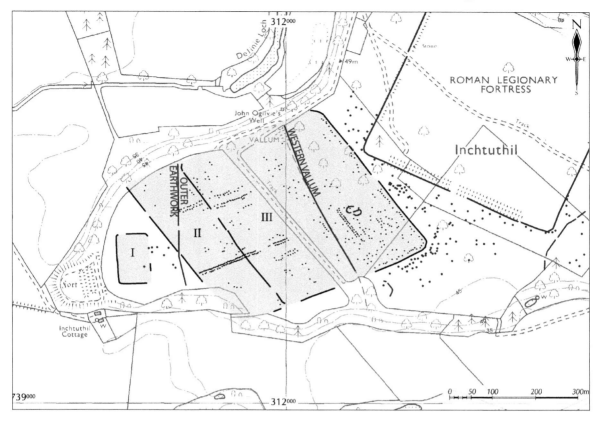

73. Plan of the fortress and camps at Inchtuthil in Perthshire.

at Crawford. Although only segments of two of the camps here are known, the current morphological characteristics of one could fit with Torwood and Beattock Barnhill to form a sequence. The possibility that these could be mid-second-century AD (Antonine) in date is exciting, given that it is currently extremely difficult to assign camps to this period due to the lack of secure dating evidence and the re-use of many neighbouring first-century AD forts in the mid-second-century AD re-conquest of southern Scotland (with the exception of those lying along the Antonine Wall – see Chapter 3). The fact that several of the camps at Beattock Barnhill could be mid-second-century AD or later indicates a significant amount of campaigning and troop movements in these periods and hints at a lack of stability in the relationship between the Roman forces and local peoples[45].

One final grouping of camps is the plethora of relatively small camps of between 0.5–2 hectares in size (1.2–5 acres) found across Britain. We have already observed the propensity for camps of around 2 hectares in size on the Antonine Wall (Chapter 3) and the annexes of around 1 hectare recorded on the camps in the 25-hectare (63-acre) series (Chapter 8). At Inchtuthil in Perthshire, a small camp of just under 1 hectare is recorded just to the west of the large camps close to the fortress (Chapter 4 and Figure 73). This location represents the best position on the whole plateau for an early small reconnaissance force and would be an odd choice if the fortress and camps were, or had been, occupied. The number of small camps now recorded across the continent as well as in Britain demonstrates that small detachments were moving around regularly, with their functions probably ranging from troops undertaking reconnaissance, to those moving between bases, to those on manoeuvres. Many lie in clusters close to other larger camps and nearby Roman forts. It is interesting to speculate that these may have held scouts (*exploratores*) gathering intelligence, but this remains pure conjecture.

It can be seen from the examples provided throughout this chapter that, although dates can sometimes be proposed for Roman camps through a variety of methods, the picture is complicated by their re-use, creating even more of a jigsaw puzzle. We don't know if an army returning from campaigns in the north and west of Britain reoccupied earlier camps or built new ones from scratch. Presumably this relies on the outward camp not being occupied for such a prolonged period that it was left in a state unsuitable for immediate re-use. If they did reoccupy one of their earlier camps, the force may have conformed to the same layout. But if a slightly different army reoccupied a camp, then it would probably opt for a different layout, and this is one possible explanation for the largely erratic interior arrangement of pits and ovens at Kintore in Aberdeenshire (Chapter 8). Or the same troops could be been internally deployed in a different disposition. Furthermore, a returning army may be a different size due to losses of troops, the division of the force into different groups possibly travelling in different directions, or the addition of prisoners.

But even with all these caveats, the fact that we can start to place occupation dates on such ephemeral and fleetingly occupied structures as temporary camps means that these sites continue to play a major role in our understanding of the Roman conquest and garrisoning of Britain.

10

Conclusions

In summary, Roman camps add much to our understanding of the conquest, occupation and other activities of the Roman army in Britain. Although elements of them remain enigmatic, not least the numbers of troops deployed within, the reasons for employing differing shapes and entrance protection, and their construction and occupation dates, we can start to tease out information, even if some of this is speculative. There is always a danger when seeking to marry up historical sources directly with archaeological evidence but as long as differences between fact and conjecture are recognised, we can start to build a picture of the campaigning army in Britain.

For example, when the Romans first invaded southern Britain through the campaigns of Julius Caesar and then the large invasion army sent by Claudius, it appears quite possible that ramparts and palisades without ditches enclosed the short-lived tented accommodations for the forces – this would help to explain the paucity of evidence for temporary camps in south-eastern England, where many of the remains have presumably been destroyed by the development of later villages, towns and cities and through centuries of ploughing. By the time that the Romans began to expand their growing province to the west and north in the mid- to late first century AD, the addition of ditches to protect the perimeters of camp sites appears to have been more widespread. The use of *claviculae* to protect entrances to camps may have been more common than hitherto suspected in the first century AD, their detection largely dependent on the survival of upstanding earthwork remains.

In AD 51 we are informed that Caratacus (formerly of the Catuvellauni tribe and now fighting with the Ordovices) had a set-piece battle with the Romans. The location of this has not been identified and the literary texts give no suggestion that siege works were constructed by the Romans, so we are merely left with searching for a Roman camp in the vicinity of an Iron Age hill-fort in Wales with a river in front[1], currently difficult to distinguish with any confidence.

Following the protracted conquest of Wales, a number of the auxiliary forts became training bases, with some upland areas giving the impression that they functioned as an ancient equivalent of the army training estate on Salisbury Plain in Wiltshire. The dating of these is unknown, but the presence of *claviculae* gates on numerous small practice camps reinforces the notion that they were constructed in the first or early second centuries AD. Although it used to be believed that only legionaries constructed camps, the location of so many practice camps outside Welsh auxiliary forts surely argues for the training of auxiliary soldiers. As they are so much more prevalent in Wales than elsewhere, it is possible that special circumstances prevailed when the area had been newly conquered, such as the training of new recruits; evidence from bronze military diplomas suggests that there was an intensive phase of recruitment in the Flavian period in the 70s and 80s AD[2]. The governor of Britain in 73/4–77 AD, Julius Frontinus, was known to have an interest in tactics and training methods and this is one potential context. By the AD 80s there is a story, recounted in Tacitus' *Agricola*, of a mutiny of a cohort of Usipi, recruited in Germany, who had been sent to Britain for training[3]. It is possible that auxiliaries were intensively trained in Wales, in advance of their deployment in northern Britain. We are informed by Tacitus that Agricola organized the auxiliaries to be at the front at the battle of Mons Graupius, to avoid legionary bloodshed[4], and the practice camps prevalent in Wales could be a remnant of auxiliary training activities at this time.

Northern Britain is where we have the most evidence for the remains of marching camps, and it was the area that remained most hostile to the invading force. Northern England and southern Scotland saw active campaigning from the late 60s AD onwards. Many marching camp remains in this area probably date from the latter half of the first century AD, although hostilities throughout the Roman occupation of Britain probably resulted in camps being constructed and/or re-occupied during later periods. If the classical sources are to be followed, these camps, in hostile territory, would have been surrounded by ditches as well as ramparts, and certainly the number and complexity of camps in northern Britain revealed through crop-markings indicating buried ditches does imply that the construction of ditches was standard practice.

Tacitus' biography of his father-in-law, the governor Agricola, has been used to tell the story of the invasions of Scotland. Although it is likely that his predecessors campaigned in southern Scotland, many of the camps in central and northern Scotland have, speculatively, been assigned to his campaigns. But even this wealth of literary evidence is not accompanied with a wealth of archaeological evidence, and we would struggle to identify anything as being 'Agricolan' if the biography had not survived. Furthermore, some of the remains in north-eastern Scotland may belong to Agricola's (unnamed) successor as governor, but at least we have fragments of dating evidence suggesting that some of these camps belonged to campaigns in the Flavian era, thereby including the period of Agricola's governorship.

Yet Tacitus' account does furnish us with other information pertinent to Roman camp studies. Agricola may have been a good general, but initiatives in the defences of camps, such as the development of 'Stracathro-type' gates, may have happened due to the desires of camp prefects rather than the involvement of the governor. Furthermore, despite the defensive precautions taken to protect camps (see Chapter 8), we are informed that, in Agricola's sixth season (AD 82) the Caledonians were able to mount a night attack on the *legio IX Hispana* and penetrate the interior of the camp[5]. Although successfully driven back by the Romans, this does highlight the need for defensive structures around overnight camping grounds. Indeed, the hostility of the tribes of Caledonia is reinforced through Tacitus' description of the set-piece battle of Mons Graupius.

Withdrawal from Scotland to the line later occupied by Hadrian's Wall may have seen either the construction of new camps or the re-occupation of earlier ones – certainly a number of camps have displayed evidence for re-use when subject to either intensive topographic earthwork survey or excavation and this may have been more commonplace than is currently supposed.

The Antonine re-conquest of southern Scotland in the mid-second century AD saw the construction and re-occupation of camps up to the isthmus between the firths of Forth and Clyde where the Antonine Wall was constructed. The army may have campaigned north of the isthmus in order to keep hostilities as far away from this new frontier as possible, with outpost forts as far as Bertha (Perth) on the River Tay. Some of the camps in this area north of the Wall must have been occupied or re-occupied in this period, and the camp at Dunning in Perthshire, with evidence for re-use and Antonine fragments of pottery (see Chapters 7 and 8), is a strong candidate. Although the group of camps enclosing some 25 hectares (63 acres) in size running from Craigarnhall in Stirling to Keithock in Angus (Figure 56) have been regularly attributed to the Severan campaigns of the early third century AD, there is no supporting archaeological evidence for this and they could also relate to campaigns in the Antonine period. Along the line of the Antonine Wall, the recurring sizes and relatively regular distribution of camps has enabled us to build a fairly convincing case for them as construction or labour camps housing the troops involved in building the frontier, thereby suggesting not only function but also date for these camps, two of which (Little Kerse and Dullatur) have provided artefactual evidence confirming their likely attribution to the Antonine period.

Whether the Antonine withdrawal from Scotland was due to hostilities in the province, possibly in south-west Scotland, is still a subject for debate, but the evidence from camps does suggest a considerable amount of troop movement in the south-west in particular, with Beattock in Dumfriesshire exhibiting multiple phases of camp construction in the mid-second century AD (see Chapter 9). This certainly implies a continued level of policing of occupied territory, providing further clues that south-west Scotland might have been troublesome. This period may be a context for a possible siege of the hill of Burnswark in Dumfriesshire (see Chapter 3) – although whether or not it was a site of a genuine siege is disputed, as is the date of such activity, the mid-second century AD remains a possibility and may be an indicator of some of the trouble that might have been encountered. The two camps on either side of the hill are the only camps in Britain which can currently lay claim to being siege camps.

After the withdrawal from Scotland and re-occupation of Hadrian's Wall, some of the camps may have been built or re-occupied during campaigns against Iron Age tribes, and bribes and payments in the form of coins and other Roman artefacts found their way to a number of Iron Age sites (such as Birnie in Moray – see Chapter 2) which lay far beyond the territory held by Rome at that point. How these objects reached such sites is not clear, but we can suggest that any movements of Roman soldiers beyond the Roman frontiers would have involved their housing in camps.

The early third-century AD campaigns of the Emperor Septimius Severus and his sons probably saw one of the largest armies to take to the field in Britain, excepting perhaps the Claudian invasion army of AD 43. Not only was this a time when the size of the garrison in northern Britain was at its greatest, but the presence of the emperor, his entourage, bodyguards and administration would have resulted in the need for the marching army to occupy large areas of ground. The large chain of marching camps of around 67 hectares (165 acres) running up Dere Street in eastern Scotland has not yet provided any secure archaeological dating evidence, but the Severan campaigns provide the most likely historical context for this chain of camps, currently among the largest known from anywhere in the Roman Empire.

After the death of Severus and the abandonment of his conquests, later campaigns into territory north of Hadrian's Wall in the third and fourth centuries AD probably saw the construction and re-occupation of camps, but these are currently archaeologically invisible. Movements of Roman soldiers around the conquered and garrisoned part of the island probably also saw construction or re-occupation of camps, reminding us that not all camps in England and Wales may be first-century AD in date. Rey Cross in County Durham (see Chapters 5 and 9) yielded late third- or early fourth-century AD pottery during excavations, indicating possible re-use at this time, and excavations at Kintore in Aberdeenshire (see Chapter 8) revealed a possible third-century AD axe head from one of the ovens and a third- or fourth-century AD Roman folded beaker from a pit[6].

The above is a speculative chronology based on our current understanding of camps in Britain. The majority of camps are interpreted as marching camps, constructed by troops on campaign or otherwise on the move. The other main functions for camps have been harder to identify: siege camps are claimed but not confirmed at Burnswark in Dumfriesshire, construction camps identified along the Antonine Wall but with limited confidence elsewhere, and practice camps were prevalent in Wales with a handful of examples also likely along Hadrian's Wall.

A glance at the current distribution of camps in Britain, particularly north of Hadrian's Wall (Figure 2), indicates a preference by the Roman forces for camping close to Roman roads and fort sites (whether sited underneath a later fort site, one demarcated for fortified occupation, or one already in use). This is hardly surprising, because these generally represent the best route ways through territory and good sites for halting for periods respectively. That the Romans had made maps of conquered territory is highly likely, and these may have taken the form of Itineraries[7] – lists of locations rather than the conventional mapping with which we are so familiar today. As noted earlier, when subjected to detailed topographical earthwork survey or excavation, a large number of camps have demonstrated that they were utilised on more than one occasion, whether this was a re-use of the entire perimeter, or a smaller area was demarcated within an existing site (such as at Pennymuir in the Scottish Borders, see Figure 35), or the area was re-used but not on the same alignment (for example, at Ardoch in Perthshire [Figures 58 and 59] and Y Pigwn in Brecknockshire [Figure 36]). This reinforces the idea that they re-used routes and returned to existing known areas of ground. This need not imply any form of temporal proximity between occupations, but merely the successful use of maps and itineraries.

Further research through geophysical survey and excavation will add much more not only to the speculative chronology outlined above but also to our understanding of the daily life of the Roman soldier on the move. Unlike legionary fortresses and auxiliary forts, we cannot identify who was housed in which camps, although legionaries and auxiliaries were regularly accommodated together in the same marching camp. Indeed, the size of many marching camps, with over 100 camps north of Hadrian's Wall enclosing in excess of 10 hectares (25 acres), stresses the collective identity of the army and the seeming archaeological invisibility of individuals and their units. It is only on very rare occasions that we can start to guess which troops constructed and were housed in specific camps. For example, we have noted above that the practice camps outside auxiliary forts in Wales may have been constructed by new recruits – this is a very rare instance when we can, on occasion, postulate which regiment(s) might have been responsible for the construction of these camps.

Outside the legionary fortresses of York and Chester, camps of a similar size and shape may have been constructed during manoeuvres by the legionaries stationed in the fortresses, although there is no evidence to support this theory and no indication of likely dates. The annexes found on the 25-hectare (63-acre) camps in Scotland are of a similar size and shape to the camps outside York and Chester (enclosing about 1 hectare – 2½ acres), and we have speculated as to their possible functions (Chapter 8). Perhaps these housed small groups of reconnaissance troops, scouts or *exploratores*, who may have been housed within the main body of the camp at other times, but for some reason camped separately when travelling with the army that occupied the 25-hectare camps. It is also possible that such annexes served for a small holding-garrison while the main body of troops were campaigning elsewhere.

When trying to discover soldiers' identities, the excavations at Kintore have provided further clues. The range of ovens recorded have very limited consistency in terms of their layout within the camp as well as their form, displaying differing orientations, sizes, construction, fuel and lining (with some being 'double' ovens). This level of variability may relate to differing preferences, diet, and ethnic origins of the troops housed within the camp. Although the majority of the ovens were probably used for baking bread, other activities such as metalworking have been identified, hinting at the routine maintenance work carried out by troops stationed away from their main bases. The discovery of carbonised wooden bowls confirms that the army carried wooden vessels as well as metal and pottery on campaign, and other metal finds may have been ripped off wooden objects, suggesting recycling of materials when necessary and potentially the burning of redundant wooden objects as fuel. A metal scythe might have been used for gathering fodder for animals, and a tethering peg is a further clue to the presence of horses or mules within the camp. We know that mules were used to carry baggage and that cavalry was deployed in the field, but evidence confirming their presence is rare. Further research and analysis at Kintore and excavations elsewhere should continue to add tantalizing information regarding the garrisons housed, length of occupation, army supply and provisions, the possible presence of camp followers, mules and wagons, indications of cavalry, the Roman military diet while on campaign and other details about the daily life of Roman forces in the field.

Kintore has exemplified the importance of large-scale excavations on Roman camps. Although small-scale trenching was the norm in the twentieth century, we have learnt so much from a single site that it is exciting to speculate as to what we might learn from other similar large-scale excavations. On a well-preserved camp, perhaps one still surviving as an earthwork, do we stand any chance of recovering lines of tent peg holes? After all, stake holes have been tentatively identified at the entrances to two camps (Castledykes in Lanarkshire and Dalginross in Perthshire) and possibly in the forward face of the rampart of a third (Galley Gill in Cumbria) (see Chapter 8). Although these probably represent the remains of palisades of some description, the discovery of a tethering peg at Kintore must leave us cautiously optimistic of finding more artefactual and possibly even structural remains from tents. Recent large-scale geophysical survey (at Dalswinton in Dumfriesshire) identified a number of ovens and pits which were not visible on the air photographs, suggesting that this could be deployed more widely to aid our understanding of camps and also select examples which would benefit from further excavation and research. Britain has the largest number of camps from any country or province in the Roman Empire, and we have benefited from more active research than any other country. We have an amazingly wealthy resource of Roman camps, from which both we and the other countries within the former Roman Empire can benefit.

Glossary of Latin and Other Terms
Used in the Text

actus: unit of length measuring 120 Roman feet

actus quadrati: two square *actus*

ala: a cavalry unit

aplekton: Byzantine term for fortified camps

auxilia: the second-line troops of the provincial armies

ballistaria: ballista platforms – firing ranges for Roman field-artillery

caltrop: device comprising four or more spikes or points arranged to rest on three spikes on the ground with the remainder pointing outwards

centuriation: method of dividing up the Roman landscape

centurion: commander of a century

century: infantry sub-unit comprising eighty soldiers

clavicula (pl. *claviculae*): a semi-circular rampart, sometimes accompanied by a ditch, constructed to expose the unshielded side of those entering the camp to the defenders

cohort: an auxiliary unit normally containing either about 500 or 1,000 soldiers or a sub-unit in a legion

contubernium (pl. *contubernia*): sub-unit of a century comprising eight soldiers who shared a tent or room – there were ten per century

denarius: small silver coin

ericus: a beam studded with spikes

exploratores: scouts or reconnaissance troops

extraordinarii: elite allies

fabrica: workshops

forum: market (or government building in a town)

glandes: lead or clay sling-bullets, possibly catapult ammunition

groma: Roman surveying instrument comprising a vertical staff with horizontal cross pieces mounted at right-angles on a bracket; each cross piece had a plumb line hanging vertically at each end

grübenhäuser: semi-subterranean Anglo-Saxon houses found in Britain and in northern Europe

horreum (pl. *horrea*): granaries

impedimenta: baggage

intervallum: space or road running between the camp perimeter and the troops *iugerum*: two square *actus* joined together – an area of 120 by 240 Roman feet

latera praetorii: the area to the side of the *praetorium*

lilia: defensive pits, as reported by Caesar during his siege of Alesia in France

limes: originally the name for a road, but later used to describe a Roman frontier

lixae: camp followers

legio: legion – comprising sixty centuries organised into ten cohorts – Roman citizens

oppidum: main tribal settlement or hill-fort

pilum murale (pl. *pila muralia*): double-pointed wooden stakes

porta decumana: the rear gate

porta praetoria: the main gate at the front of the camp

porta principalis dextra: the side gate on the right hand side of the camp

porta principalis sinistra: the side gate on the left hand side of the camp

praefectus castrorum: camp prefect

praetorium: general's tent/commanding officer's house

praetentura: the area in front of the *praetorium*

principia: headquarters buildings

quaestor: junior magistrate in charge of the legion's affairs

quaestorium: office of the *quaestor*

retentura: the area behind the *praetorium*

Stracathro-type: entrance protection to a camp comprising an external *clavicula* rampart and ditch with an oblique ditch (possibly accompanied by a rampart); probably also accompanied by an internal curving rampart

titulus (pl. *tituli*): a short stretch of rampart and ditch, set forward from the entrance gap, providing an obstacle to be navigated by all camp entrants

traiectus: crossing

tribune: legionary officer (of which there were six per legion) or commander of a 1,000-strong auxiliary unit

turma (pl. *turmae*): cavalry sub-unit of around thirty-two men (the cavalry equivalent of a century)

valetudinarium: hospital

vallus (pl. *valli*): sharpened stake

via praetoria: the road running to the main entrance of the camp

via principalis: the road running to the two side gates of the camp

via quintana: the road behind the *praetorium*, parallel to the *via principalis*

via sagularis: the road running around the camp, between the legionary cohorts encamped around the edge of the camp and the troops quartered further within

Further Reading

As stated in the preface, the three volumes on Roman camps produced for England, Wales and Scotland provide the best starting point for information about camps in those three countries and references to other sources (only some of which are listed in this book):

Welfare, H. and Swan, V. 1995. *Roman Camps in England. The Field Archaeology*. RCHME, London.
Davies, J. L. and Jones, R. H. 2006. *Roman Camps in Wales and the Marches*. University of Wales Press, Cardiff.
Jones, R. H. forthcoming 2011. *Roman Camps in Scotland*. Society of Antiquaries of Scotland, Edinburgh.

CLASSICAL SOURCES

Classical texts are available in translation in the Loeb Classical Library series published by Harvard University Press. Many are also available in other series, notably the Penguin Classics. Where other translations have been used, these are stated. Other translations of specific passages relating to Roman Britain can be found in Ireland 1986, and to the Roman army in Campbell 1994.

Ammianus Marcellinus
Appian – *Iberica* (History of Rome: The Spanish Wars)
Caesar – *de Bello Gallico* (The Gallic War)
Caesar – *de Bello Civili* (The Civil War)
Cassius Dio – Roman History
Eutropius – *Breviarium historiae Romanae* (Abridgement of Roman History)
Frontinus – *Strategemata* (Stratagems)
Herodian – History of the Empire
Hyginus Gromaticus – *de limitibus constituendis* (The Boundaries)
Hyginus – *de munitionibus castrorum* (The Fortification of the Camp) (Gilliver 1993a)
Josephus – *Bellum Iudaicum* (The Jewish War)
Libanus – *Oration* (Ireland 1986)
Livy – History of Rome
Maurice – *Strategikon* (Handbook of Byzantine Military Strategy) (Dennis 1984)
Onasander – *Strategikos* (On Generalship)
Plutarch – *Pyrrhus* (The Life of Pyrrhus)
Polybius – Histories
Sallust – *de Bello Jugurtha* (The Jugurthine War)
Scriptores Historiae Augustae – *Hadrian* (Ireland 1986)
Strabo – *Geographica*
Suetonius – *Vespasian* (The Twelve Caesars: Vespasian)
Tacitus – *Agricola* (Birley 1999)
Tacitus – *Annals*

Tacitus – *Histories*
Valerius Maximus – *Facta et dicta memorabilia* (Memorable Sayings and Doings)
Vegetius – *Epitoma Rei Militaris* (Epitome of Military Science) (Milner 1996)
Vitruvius – *de Architectura* (On Architecture)
Xenophon – The Education of Cyrus

MODERN SOURCES

Aharoni, Y. 1961. 'The Caves of Nahal Hever', *'Atiqot'. Journal of the Israel Department of Antiquities* III: 148–162.

Austin, N. J. E. and Rankov, N. B. 1995. *Exploratio. Military and Political Intelligence in the Roman World from the Second Punic War to the Battle of Adrianople*. London, Routledge.

Bailey, G. B. 2000. 'Excavations on the Roman temporary camps at the Three Bridges, Camelon, Falkirk', *Proceedings of the Society of Antiquaries of Scotland* 130: 469–489.

Bennett, J. 1982. 'The Great Chesters "Pilum Murale"', *Archaeologia Aeliana* (Fifth series) X: 200-205.

Birley, A. R. 1999. *Tacitus. Agricola and Germany*. Oxford, Oxford World's Classics, Oxford University Press.

Birley, E. 1936. 'Three notes on Roman Wales', *Archaeologia Cambrensis* XCI: 58–73.

Birley, E. 1966. '"Alae' and 'Cohortes Milliariae"', in *Corolla Memoriae Erich Swoboda Dedicata (Romische Forschungen in Niederosterreich V)*. Cologne: 54–67.

Birley, E. 1982. 'The Dating and Character of the tract 'de munitionibus castrorum"', in Wirth, G. (ed.) *Romanitas-Christianitas. Untersuchungen zu Geschichte und Literatur der römischen Kaiserzeit*. Berlin and New York: 277–281.

Birley, R. 2009. *Vindolanda. A Roman Frontier Fort on Hadrian's Wall*. Amberley, Stroud.

Bowman, A. K. and Thomas, J. D. 1991. 'A Military Strength Report from Vindolanda', *Journal of Roman Studies* LXXXI: 62–73.

Bowman, A. K. and Thomas, J. D. 1994. *The Vindolanda Writing Tablets (Tabulae Vindolandenses II)*. London, British Museum Press.

Breeze, D. J. 1984a. 'Demand and Supply on the Northern Frontier', in Miket, R. and Burgess, C. (eds) *Between and Beyond the Walls: Essays on the Prehistory and History of North Britain in Honour of George Jobey*, Edinburgh: 264–86.

Breeze, D. J. 1984b. 'The Roman Fort on the Antonine Wall at Bearsden', in Breeze, D. J. (ed.) *Studies in Scottish Antiquity presented to Stewart Cruden*. John Donald, Edinburgh: 32–68.

Breeze, D. J. 1988. 'The Logistics of Agricola's Final Campaign', *Talanta, Dutch Archaeological and Historical Journal* 18/19: 7–22.

Breeze, D. J. 2006a. *The Antonine Wall*. Birlinn, Edinburgh.

Breeze, D. J. 2006b. *Handbook to the Roman Wall*, fourteenth edition. Newcastle upon Tyne, The Society of Antiquaries of Newcastle upon Tyne.

Breeze, D. J. 2011. *The Frontiers of Imperial Rome*. Pen & Sword, Barnsley.

Breeze, D. J. and Dobson, B. 2000. *Hadrian's Wall*, fourth edition. Penguin, London.

Burnham, B. C. and Davies, J. L. 2010. (eds) *Roman Frontiers in Wales and the Marches*. Royal Commission on the Ancient and Historical Monuments of Wales, Aberystwyth.

Callander, J. G. 1919. 'Notes on the Roman remains at Grassy Walls, and Bertha near Perth', *Proceedings of the Society of Antiquaries of Scotland* 53: 137–152.

Camden, W. 1790. *Britannia*. (Gough's edition). Oxford.

Campbell, B 1994 *The Roman Army, 31 BC – AD 337. A Sourcebook*. London, Routledge.

Campbell, D. B. 2003. 'The Roman Siege of Burnswark', *Britannia* XXXIV: 19–33.

Caruana, I. D. 1992. 'Carlisle: Excavation of a Section of the Annexe Ditch of the First Flavian Fort, 1990', *Britannia* XXIII: 45–109.

Charlton, B. and Day, J. 1984 'Henry MacLauchlan: Surveyor and Field Archaeologist' in Miket, R. and Burgess, C. (eds) *Between and Beyond the Walls: Essays on the Prehistory and History of North Britain in Honour of George Jobey*, Edinburgh: 4–37.

Collingwood, R. G. and Richmond, I. 1969. *The Archaeology of Roman Britain* (revised edition). London.

Collingwood, R. G. and Wright, R. P. 1995. *The Roman Inscriptions of Britain. Volume I: Inscriptions on Stone. Addenda and Corrigenda by R. S. O. Tomlin.* Stroud, Sutton.

Cook, M. and Dunbar, L. 2008. *Rituals, Roundhouses and Romans: Excavations at Kintore, Aberdeenshire 2000-2006. Volume 1. Forest Road.* Edinburgh, Scottish Trust for Archaeological Research Monograph 8.

Coulston, J. C. N. forthcoming. *All the Emperor's Men. Roman Soldiers and Barbarians on Trajan's Column*, Oxbow Publishing, Oxford.

Crawford, O. G. S. 1949. *Topography of Roman Scotland, North of the Antonine Wall.* Cambridge, Cambridge University Press.

Davies, G. 2006. *Roman Siege Works.* Tempus, Stroud.

Dennis, G. T. 1984. *Maurice's Strategikon. Handbook of Byzantine Military Strategy.* University of Pennsylvania Press, Philadelphia.

Dilke, O. A. W. 1971. *The Roman land surveyors.* Newton Abbot.

Dobson, B. 1981. 'Agricola's Life and Career', *Scottish Archaeological Forum* 12: 1–13.

Dobson, M. 2008. *The Army of the Roman Republic. The second century BC, Polybius and the Camps at Numantia, Spain.* Oxbow, Oxford.

Dunwell, A. J. and Keppie, L. J. F. 1995. 'The Roman Temporary Camp at Dunning, Perthshire: Evidence from two Recent Excavations', *Britannia* XXVI: 51–62.

Fabricius, E. 1932. 'Some Notes on Polybius's Description of Roman Camps', *Journal of Roman Studies* XXII: 78–87.

Feachem, R. W. 1970. 'Mons Craupius = Duncrub?', *Antiquity* XLIV: 120–124.

Fraser, J. E. 2005. *The Roman Conquest of Scotland. The Battle of Mons Graupius AD 84.* Stroud, Tempus.

Frere, S. S. 1985a. 'C. The Garrisons of the Camps', in Pitts, L. F. and St Joseph, J. K. *Inchtuthil. The Roman Legionary Fortress.* London, Britannia Monograph Series 6: 239–244.

Frere, S. S. 1985b. 'B. The Pits: Discussion', in Pitts, L. F. and St Joseph, J. K. *Inchtuthil. The Roman Legionary Fortress.* London, Britannia Monograph Series 6: 229–239.

Frere, S. S. and St Joseph, J. K. S. 1983. *Roman Britain from the Air.* Cambridge, Cambridge University Press.

Frere, S. S. and Tomlin, R. S. O. 1990–5. *The Roman Inscriptions of Britain. Volume II: Fascicules 1–8.* Stroud, Sutton.

Frere, S. S. and Wilkes, J. J. 1989. *Strageath. Excavations within the Roman fort 1973-86.* London, Britannia Monograph Series 9.

Fulford, M. 2000. 'The Organization of legionary supply: the Claudian invasion of Britain', in Brewer, R. J. (ed.) 2000, *Roman Fortresses and their Legions*, Society of Antiquaries and National Museums and Galleries of Wales, London/Cardiff: 41–50.

Gates, T. and Ainsworth, S. 2008. 'A Newly Identified Roman Temporary Camp at Cow Close, near Bowes, Co. Durham,' *Britannia* XXXIX: 240–5.

Gilliver, C. M .1993a .'The *de munitionibus castrorum*: Text and Translation', *Journal of Roman Military Equipment Studies* 4: 33–48.

Gilliver, C. M. 1993b. 'Hedgehogs, caltrops and palisade stakes', *Journal of Roman Military Equipment Studies* 4: 49–54.

Gilliver, C. M. 1999. *The Roman Art of War.* Stroud, Tempus.

Grillone, A. 1977. *Hyginus de metatione castrorum.* Leipzig.

Halliday, S. P. 1982. 'Later prehistoric farming in South-Eastern Scotland', in Harding, D. W. (ed.) *Later Prehistoric Settlement in South-East Scotland*, University of Edinburgh, Department of Archaeology, Occasional Paper No 8: 74–91.

Hanson, W. S. 1978. 'Roman campaigns north of the Forth-Clyde isthmus: the evidence of the temporary camps', *Proceedings of the Society of Antiquaries of Scotland* 109: 140–150.

Hanson, W. S. 1991. *Agricola and the Conquest of the North.* (Second edition.) London, Batsford.

Hanson, W. S. 2007. *Elginhaugh: a Flavian fort and its annexe.* London, Britannia Monograph Series.

Hanson, W. S. and Maxwell, G. S. 1986. *Rome's north-west frontier: The Antonine Wall.* Edinburgh, Edinburgh University Press.

Hill, P. 2006. *The Construction of Hadrian's Wall*, Stroud.

Hodgson, N. 2009. 'The abandonment of Antonine Scotland: its date and causes' in Hanson, W. S. (ed.) *The army and frontiers of Rome*. Journal of Roman Archaeology Supplementary series 74, Portsmouth, Rhode Island: 185–93.

Holder, P. 1982. *The Roman Army in Britain*, Batsford, London.

Horn, H. G. 1987. *Die Romer in Nordrhein-Westfalen*, Konrad Theiss, Stuttgart.

Hughes, G., Leach, P. and Stanford, S. C. 1995. 'Excavations at Bromfield, Shropshire, 1981-1991', *Transactions of the Shropshire Archaeological and Historical Society* 70: 23–94.

Hunter, F. 2002. 'Native power and Roman politics. An Iron Age settlement and Roman coin hoards at Birnie, Moray', *History Scotland* 2 (4): 22–28.

Hunter, F. 2007. *Beyond the Edge of Empire – Caledonians, Picts and Romans*. Groam House Museum.

Hunter, F. forthcoming. 'The Roman finds from Kintore in context', in Cook, M. J., Dunbar, L. and Heawood, R. forthcoming *Rituals, Roundhouses and Romans: Excavations at Kintore, Aberdeenshire 2000-2006. Volume 2, Other Sites*. Edinburgh, Scottish Trust for Archaeological Research Monograph.

Ireland, S 1986 *Roman Britain. A Sourcebook*. London, Routledge.

Jameson, Revd 1786. 'An Account of the Roman Camps of Battle Dykes and Haerfauds, with the Via Militaris extending between them, in the County of Forfar', in Nichols, J. *Bibliotheca Topographica Britannica* V: 16–26. London.

Johnston, D. A. 1994. 'Carronbridge, Dumfries and Galloway: the excavation of Bronze Age cremations, Iron Age settlements and a Roman camp', *Proceedings of the Society of Antiquaries of Scotland* 124: 233–291.

Jones, R. H. 2005a. 'Temporary camps on the Antonine Wall', in Visy, Z. (ed.) *Limes XIX. Proceedings of the XIXth International Congress of Roman Frontier Studies held in Pécs, Hungary, September 2003*. Pécs, University of Pécs: 551–560.

Jones, R. H. 2005b. 'The advantages of bias in Roman studies', in Brophy, K. and Cowley, D. C. (eds) *From the Air: Understanding Aerial Archaeology*: 86–93. Stroud, Tempus.

Jones, R. H. 2009a. 'Troop movements in Scotland: the evidence from marching camps', in Morillo, A., Hanel, N. and Martín, E. (eds) *Limes XX: Estudios sobre la Frontera Romana / Roman Frontier Studies*, Anejos de *Gladius* 13, Madrid: 867–78.

Jones, R. H. 2009b. '"Lager mit *claviculae*" in *Britannia*', in Hanson, W. S. (ed.) *The army and frontiers of Rome*. Journal of Roman Archaeology Supplementary series 74, Portsmouth, Rhode Island: 11–24.

Jones, R. H. and McKeague, P. 2009. 'A 'Stracathro'-gated temporary camp at Raeburnfoot, Dumfriesshire, Scotland', *Britannia* XL: 113–26.

Jones, R. H. and Maxwell, G. S. 2008. 'A Horseman Riding by: Archaeological Discovery in 1754', *Tayside and Fife Archaeological Journal* 14: 1–8.

Keppie, L. J. F. 1984. *The Making of the Roman Army from Republic to Empire*. London.

Keppie, L. J. F. 2009. 'Burnswark Hill: native space and Roman invaders,' in Hanson, W. S. (ed.) *The army and frontiers of Rome*. Journal of Roman Archaeology Supplementary series 74, Portsmouth, Rhode Island: 241–52.

Kennedy, D. L. and Riley, D. N. 1990. *Rome's Desert Frontier from the Air*. London.

Lenoir, M. 1977. 'Lager mit Clavicvlae', *Melanges de l'ecole Francais de Rome: Antiquite* 89: 697–722.

Lenoir, M. 1979. *Pseudo-Hygin, des Fortifications du camp*. Paris.

Lepper, F. and Frere, S. 1988. *Trajan's Column*. Gloucester, Alan Sutton.

Macdonald, G. 1916. 'The Roman Camps at Raedykes and Glenmailen', *Proceedings of the Society of Antiquaries of Scotland* 50: 317–359.

MacLauchlan, H. 1852. *Memoir written during a survey of the Watling Street, from the Tees to the Scotch border, in the years 1850 and 1851*. London.

MacLauchlan, H. 1857. *The Roman Wall. And illustrations of the principal vestiges of Roman occupation in the North of England. Consisting of plans of the military works, the stations, camps, ancient ways, and other remains of the earlier periods, in the Northern Counties*. London.

Maitland, W. 1757. *History and Antiquities of Scotland*. London.

Mann, J. C. 1985. 'Two 'Topoi' in the Agricola', *Britannia* XVI: 21–4.

Maxfield, V. A. 1975. 'Excavations at Eskbank, Midlothian, 1972', *Proceedings of the Society of Antiquaries of Scotland* 105: 141–150.

Maxfield, V. A. 2009. ''Where did they put the men?' An enquiry into the accommodation of soldiers in Roman Egypt', in Hanson, W. S. (ed.) *The army and frontiers of Rome*. Journal of Roman Archaeology Supplementary series 74, Portsmouth, Rhode Island: 63–82.

Maxwell, G. S. 1981. 'Agricola's Campaigns: The Evidence of the Temporary Camps', *Scottish Archaeological Forum* 12: 25–54.

Maxwell, G. S. 1982. 'Roman temporary camps at Inchtuthill: an examination of the aerial photographic evidence', *Scottish Archaeological Review* I (2): 105–113.

Maxwell, G. S. 1989. *The Romans in Scotland*. Edinburgh, The Mercat Press.

Maxwell, G. S. 1990. *A Battle Lost: Romans and Caledonians at Mons Graupius*. Edinburgh, Edinburgh University Press.

Maxwell, G. S. 1998. *A Gathering of Eagles: Scenes from Roman Scotland*. Edinburgh, The Making of Scotland Series, Canongate.

Maxwell, G. S. 2004. 'The Roman Penetration of the North in the Late First Century AD', in Todd, M. (ed.) *A Companion to Roman Britain*: 75–90. Oxford, Blackwell.

Miller, M. 1975. 'Stilicho's Pictish War,' *Britannia* VI: 141–145.

Miller, M. C. J. and DeVoto, J. G. 1994. *Polybius and Pseudo-Hyginus: The Fortification of the Roman Camp*. Chicago, Ares.

Milner, N. P. 1996. *Vegetius: Epitome of Military Science* (Second edition). Liverpool, Liverpool University Press.

Morillo, Á. M. 2003. 'Los establecimientos militares temporales: conquista y defensa del territorio en la Hispania republicana', in Morillo, Á., Cadiou, F. and Hourcade, D. *Defensa y territorio en Hispania de los Escipiones a Augusto*, León, Spain: 41–80.

Neighbour, T. 1998. 'Excavations on the Roman temporary camp at Longforgan, near Dundee, 1994', *Tayside and Fife Archaeological Journal* 4: 99–105.

Ogilvie, R. M. and Richmond, I. A. 1967. *Tacitus: Agricola*. Oxford, Oxford University Press.

Ordnance Survey. 1956. *Map of Roman Britain*. Third edition, Southampton.

Ordnance Survey. 2001. *Map of Roman Britain*. Fifth edition, Southampton.

Peddie, J. 1987. *Conquest. The Roman Invasion of Britain*. Stroud, Sutton Publishing.

Philpott, R. A. 1998. 'New Evidence from Aerial Reconnaissance for Roman Military Sites in Cheshire', *Britannia* XXIX: 341–353.

Price, T. 1814. 'An Account of some Roman Remains near Llandrindod', *Archaeologia* XVII: 168–172.

Raisen, P. and Rees, T. 1996. 'Excavation of three crop-mark sites at Melville Nurseries, Dalkeith', *Glasgow Archaeological Journal* 19: 31–50.

RCAHMS. 1956. *An inventory of the ancient and historical monuments of Roxburghshire with the fourteenth report of the Commission*. Edinburgh.

RCAHMS. 1957. *An inventory of the ancient and historical monuments of Selkirkshire with the fifteenth report of the Commission*. Edinburgh.

RCAHMS. 1997. *Eastern Dumfriesshire: an archaeological landscape*. Edinburgh.

RCAHMW. 1976. *An Inventory of the Ancient Monuments in Glamorgan. Volume I: Pre-Norman. Part II. The Iron Age and the Roman Occupation*, HMSO, Cardiff.

Reddé, M. 1995. '*Titulum* et *Clavicula* à propos des fouilles récentes d'Alésia', *Revue Archéologique de l'Est* 46.2: 349–356.

Reed, N. 1976. 'The Scottish campaigns of Septimius Severus', *Proceedings of the Society of Antiquaries of Scotland* 107: 92–102.

Richardson, A. 2000. 'The numerical basis of Roman camps', *Oxford Journal of Archaeology* 19(4): 425–437.

Richmond, I. A. 1932. 'The four Roman camps at Cawthorn in the North Riding of Yorkshire', *Archaeological Journal* 89: 17–78.

Richmond, I. A. 1962. 'The Roman Siege-works of Masada, Israel', *Journal of Roman Studies* LII: 142–155.

Richmond, I. A. 1982. *Trajan's Army on Trajan's Column*. Preface and bibliography by Mark Hassall. London, The British School at Rome.

Richmond, I. A. and Keeney, G. S. 1937. 'The Roman works at Chew Green, Coquetdalehead', *Archaeologia Aeliana* (Fourth series) XIV: 129–150.

Richmond, I. A. and McIntyre, J. 1934 'The Roman Camps at Rey Cross and Crackenthorpe', *Transactions of the Cumberland and Westmorland Antiquarian and Archaeological Society* 34: 50–61.

Richmond, I. A. and St Joseph, J. K. S. 1982. 'Excavations at Woden Law, 1950', *Proceedings of the Society of Antiquaries of Scotland* 112: 277–84.

Robertson, A. S. 1980. 'The bridges on Severan coins of AD 208 and 209', in Hanson, W. S. and Keppie, L. J. F. (eds) *Roman Frontier Studies 1979: papers presented to the Twelfth International Congress of Roman Frontier Studies*, Oxford, British Archaeological Reports International Series 71: 131–140.

Rodríguez Martín, G. and Gorges, J. G. 2006. 'El Pedrosillo Battlefield?', in Morillo, A. and Aurrecoechea, J. (eds) *The Roman Army in Hispania: an archaeological guide*. León, Spain: 263–8.

Rogers, I. M. 1993. 'Dalginross and Dun: excavations at two Roman camps', *Proceedings of the Society of Antiquaries of Scotland* 123: 277–290.

Roxan, M. 1978. *Roman Military Diplomas 1954-1977*. London: Institute of Archaeology, London Occasional Publication 2.

Roy, W. 1793. *The Military Antiquities of the Romans in Britain*. London, Soc. of Antiq.

Salvatore, J. P. 1996. *Roman Republican Castrametation. A reappraisal of historical and archaeological sources*. Oxford, British Archaeol Reports International Series 630.

Schlüter, W. 1999. 'The Battle of the Teutoburg Forest: archaeological research at Kelkreise near Osnabruck', in Creighton, J. D. and Wilson, R. J. A. (eds) *Roman Germany. Studies in Cultural Interaction*. Journal of Roman Archaeology Supplementary series 32: 125–159. Portsmouth, Rhode Island.

Scollar, I. 1965. *Archäologie aus der Luft*. Dusseldorf, Rheinland-Verlag.

St Joseph, J. K. 1976. 'Air Reconnaissance of Roman Scotland, 1939-75', *Glasgow Archaeological Journal* 4: 1–28.

St Joseph, J. K. 1978. 'The camp at Durno, Aberdeenshire, and the site of Mons Graupius', *Britannia* IX: 271–288.

Stefan, A. S. 1997. 'Les guerres Daciques de Trajan: les opérations du front Alpin', in Groenman-van Waateringe, W., van Beek, B. L ., Willems, W. J. H., and Wynia, S. L. (eds) *Roman Frontier Studies 1995*. Oxford, Oxbow Monographs 91: 517–525.

Steer, K. A. and Feachem, R. W. 1954. 'The Roman fort and temporary camp at Oakwood, Selkirkshire', *Proceedings of the Society of Antiquaries of Scotland* 86: 81–105.

Strachan, R. 1999. 'Easter Moss, Cowie (St Ninians parish), evaluation; souterrain,' *Discovery and Excavation in Scotland*: 88.

Swan, V. G. 1999. 'The Twentieth Legion and the history of the Antonine Wall reconsidered', *Proceedings of the Society of Antiquaries of Scotland* 129: 399–480.

Thomas, J. and Constantinides Hero, A. (eds.) 2000 *Byzantine Monastic Foundation Documents: A Complete Translation of the Surviving Founders' Typika and Testaments*. Washington: Dumbarton Oaks.

Tipping, R. 1997. 'The Environmental History of the Landscape', in RCAHMS. *Eastern Dumfriesshire: an archaeological landscape*: 10–25. Edinburgh, TSO.

Tomlin, R. S. O., Wright, R. P. and Hassall, M. W. C. 2009. *Roman Inscriptions of Britain Volume III: Inscriptions on Stone (1955-2006)*. Oxford.

Visy, Z. 2003. *The Ripa Pannonica in Hungary*. Budapest, Akademiai Kiado.

Wells, P. S. 2003. *The Battle that Stopped Rome. Emperor Augustus, Arminius, and the slaughter of the legions in the Teutoburger forest*. New York, W.W. Norton.

Williams, J. 1856. 'History of Radnorshire. Section 6 – Roman Stations and Roads', *Archaeologia Cambrensis* 3rd ser. Vol II: 24–39.

List of Illustrations

2. Aerial view across to Bennachie in Aberdeenshire. © Crown Copyright: RCAHMS. SC872649. Licensor www.rcahms.gov.uk

3. View of one of the siege camps at Numantia (Peña Redonda) in north-west Spain. Photograph taken in 2006.

4. Aerial view of the Roman construction camp at Tamfourhill, on the Antonine Wall in Stirlingshire. © Crown Copyright: RCAHMS. SC908888. Licensor www.rcahms.gov.uk

5. Aerial view of the Antonine Wall camps at Dullatur in Lanarkshire, under excavation in 1998. © Crown Copyright: RCAHMS. SC872940. Licensor www.rcahms.gov.uk

6. Reconstruction of a *groma* from Carnuntum in Austria. Photograph taken in 2005.

7. Photograph of Trajan's Column in Rome. Photograph taken in 2006.

8. Aerial view of the marching camp at Hindwell Farm in Radnorshire. © Crown Copyright: Royal Commission on the Ancient and Historical Monuments of Wales. 895504.15.

9. LiDAR image of the new camp at Carrawburgh, lying to the south-west of the Carrawburgh fort (Latin: Brocolitia) on Hadrian's Wall. © English Heritage; LiDAR source Cambridge University Unit for Landscape Modelling (March 2004).

10. View of a section of upstanding rampart and ditch surviving in Whig Street Wood at Kirkbuddo in Angus. Photograph taken in 2004.

11. View of a reconstructed palisade on top of a marching camp rampart, Carnuntum, Austria. Photograph taken in 2005.

12. View of a reconstruction of a section of the defences of a Roman marching camp with a 'caltrop' palisade at Archaeolink Prehistory Park, Aberdeenshire. Photograph taken in 2004.

13. View of one of the external *clavicula* gates of the camp at Cawthorn in North Yorkshire. Photograph taken in 2009.

14. Aerial view of the camp at Dalginross in Perthshire. © Crown Copyright: RCAHMS. SC624586. Licensor www.rcahms.gov.uk

15. Detailed three-dimensional contour model of the north-west gate at Raeburnfoot, surveyed using a differential Global Positioning System and with a x3 exaggeration. © Crown Copyright: RCAHMS. Licensor www.rcahms.gov.uk

16. View of a reconstructed tent from Archaeolink Prehistory Park, Aberdeenshire. Photograph taken in 2004.

17. View of a reconstructed Roman oven from the Saalburg in Germany. Photograph taken in 2004.

18. View of a reconstructed Roman oven from Archaeolink Prehistory Park, Aberdeenshire. Photograph taken in 2004.

19. Aerial view of the camp at Dun in Perthshire. © Crown Copyright: RCAHMS. DP050510. Licensor www.rcahms.gov.uk

20. Aerial view of the Roman fort at Ardoch in Perthshire, taken from the north under snow cover in 1984. © Crown Copyright: RCAHMS. SC337315. Licensor www.rcahms.gov.uk

21. Aerial view of the Roman fort and camps at Newstead, taken from the north-east in 2006. © Crown Copyright: RCAHMS. DP019895. Licensor www.rcahms.gov.uk

Endnotes

CHAPTER 1 – INTRODUCTION

1. For Roman frontiers, also see Breeze 2011
2. Welfare and Swan 1995; Davies and Jones 2006; Jones forthcoming 2011
3. Bowman and Thomas 1991; 1994 and online at http://vindolanda.csad.ox.ac.uk/
4. Ireland 1986
5. Collingwood and Wright 1995; Tomlin, Wright and Hassall 2009; various fascicules of Roman inscriptions on objects other than stone including domestic utensils (*The Roman Inscriptions of Britain Volume II*) edited by Frere and Tomlin

CHAPTER 2 – THE ROMAN CONQUEST OF BRITAIN

1. Caesar *de Bello Gallico*
2. Caesar *de Bello Gallico* V, 14
3. Strabo IV, 5, 2
4. Tacitus *Agricola*, 13 (Birley 1999); also see chapter 4
5. Suetonius *Vespasian* 4
6. Tacitus *Annals* XII, 31
7. The Silures appear to have occupied a substantial area in south Wales, the Ordovices in north Wales
8. Tacitus *Agricola* 17
9. Tacitus *Agricola* 18
10. Tacitus *Agricola* 29ff
11. An excellent discussion of the search for Mons Graupius can be found in Maxwell 1990
12. Feachem 1970; Fraser 2005
13. St Joseph 1978
14. Wells 2003
15. Also see Hunter 2007
16. Eutropius VII, 13, 3
17. Tacitus *Histories* I.2
18. Breeze and Dobson 2000, 14
19. Scriptores Historiae Augustae *Hadrian* V, 1–2, written in around the fourth century AD
20. Cassius Dio LXXII.8
21. RIB 3512: Tomlin, Wright and Hassall 2009, 458–62
22. Cassius Dio LXXV.5.4
23. Hunter 2002
24. Herodian III, 14, 1
25. Cassius Dio LXXVI.13
26. *Pan. Lat. Vet*: vi (vii) 7, 1–2 (see Ireland 1986); Ammianus Marcellinus XX.1; Miller 1975
27. Libanus *Oration* 59.139,141

CHAPTER 3 – WHAT IS A ROMAN CAMP?

1. Frere and Wilkes 1989, 117
2. See Davies 2006

3. Davies and Jones 2006, 156–9
4. RCAHMS 1956, 169–72; Richmond and St Joseph 1982; Halliday 1982, 80–3
5. Welfare and Swan 1995, 137–42
6. For a more detailed discussion of Burnswark, see RCAHMS 1997, 179–82; Campbell 2003; Keppie 2009; and Jones forthcoming 2011, 154–6
7. For a reconstruction, see Maxwell 1998, 46–9
8. Campbell 2003
9. RCAHMS 1997, 179–82
10. Davies 2006, 47–8, 58–9
11. Davies 2006, 39, 47
12. For further discussion of Antonine Wall camps, see Hanson and Maxwell 1986, 118–9; Jones 2005a
13. Jones 2005a
14. Jones forthcoming 2011, 303–4
15. Vitruvius, *De Architectura*, II, V
16. Davies and Jones 2006, 67–90
17. Appian, *Iberica*, 86
18. Davies and Jones 2006, 176–85
19. Davies and Jones 2006; 187–94
20. Welfare and Swan 1995, 24
21. Philpott 1998; Davies and Jones 2006, 143–6
22. Welfare and Swan 1995, 135–6
23. Information on continental camps can be found in a variety of sources. For these sites this includes Horn 1987, 333; Scollar 1965; Visy 2003, 34–8. A brief discussion of these is in Davies and Jones 2006, 74–5
24. Tacitus *Annals* XIII, 34–5
25. Davies and Jones 2006, 60, 148–9
26. Tacitus *Annals* I.49

CHAPTER 4 – HISTORICAL SOURCES
1. Gilliver 1999
2. Frontinus *Strategemata* IV.I.14; Livy XXXV.14; Plutarch *Pyrrhus* XVI.4–5
3. Noted by Gilliver 1999, 67, fig. 67
4. For example, the writings of the Greek historian Xenophon, writing between the fifth and fourth centuries BC: *The Education of Cyrus* VIII.5.1–16
5. Hyginus Gromaticus *de limitibus constituendis* 12 (this is believed to be a different author from the Hyginus who wrote *de munitionibus castrorum*); also see note 15.
6. Vegetius *Epitoma* I.21
7. Polybius VI.19–42
8. Keppie 1984, 44–51
9. Roy 1793, 41–54, Pl. IV
10. For example, see Dobson 2008
11. Keppie 1984, 33; Gilliver 1999, 16
12. Such as Vegetius' *Epitoma Rei Militaris*, see Milner 1996, xiii–xxxi. Gilliver (1999, 173) comments that Cato the Elder may have been the first Roman to compile a military treatise, and although his *de Re Militari* has not survived, it may have been one of the manuals used by Polybius. Gilliver further lists all the important Roman military treatises which have survived or are known from antiquity (1999, 173–7).
13. Tacitus *Agricola* 17–18
14. Davies and Jones 2006
15. This is believed to be a different author to the Hyginus Gromaticus who wrote *de limitibus constituendis*; also see note 5
16. For example, Birley 1966; 1982
17. Lenoir 1979, 111; Gilliver 1993a, 33; Miller and DeVoto 1994, 61–2
18. Milner 1996, xli
19. Vegetius *Epitoma* I.21; III.10
20. Milner 1996, xvii
21. For example, Hanson 1978; Ireland 1986
22. Hunter forthcoming
23. Vegetius *Epitoma* I.21–25; III.8
24. Maurice *Strategikon* XII.B.22; XII.C

25. Thomas and Constantinides Hero 2000, 1679
26. Onasander *Strategikos*
27. Josephus *Bellum Iudaicum* III.72–109
28. Caesar *de Bello Gallico* VII.72–3
29. Sallust *de Bello Jugurtha* XLIV–XLV
30. For example, Valerius Maximus in his 'Memorable Sayings and Doings' – *Facta et dicta memorabilia* II.7
31. For example, Richmond 1982; Lepper and Frere 1988; Coulston forthcoming

CHAPTER 5 – LAYOUT AND HOLDING CAPACITY

1. Fabricius 1932
2. Polybius VI.27-34
3. During excavations in the area, the original excavators of the camp of Renieblas III attempted to identify this camp as conforming to the Polybian layout, but this has not garnered universal acceptance – also see Dobson 2008; Salvatore 1996, and Keppie 1984, 37, 44-6, 236
4. For example, those described by Hyginus; see Chapter 4
5. Sallust *de Bello Jugurtha* XLIV–XLV; Valerius Maximus *Facta et dicta memorabilia* II.7.1–2
6. Appian *Iberica* 85
7. Caesar *de Bello Gallico* VI.36–7
8. Vegetius *Epitome* III, 6
9. Hyginus *de munitionibus castrorum* 1–2, 8–19; see Chapter 4
10. For example Gilliver 1993a. Gilliver (1999, 84-7) has also applied Hyginian methodology to hypothetical reconstructions of the camps at Rey Cross (County Durham) and Logie Durno (Aberdeenshire), proposing an army of 8,640 at the former and 53,532 at the latter. While an interesting exercise, the lack of any corroborating evidence ensures that it remains purely speculative
11. Vegetius *Epitoma* I.22, III.8; see Chapter 4
12. For example, Frontinus *Strategemata* I.I.9, II.V.17, II.XII.4; Onasander's writings of the duties of a general: *Strategikos* X.13, X.19
13. Onasander *Strategikos* VIII.2; see Chapter 4
14. Vegetius *Epitoma* I. 21; III. 2; Hyginus *de munitionibus castrorum* 57; see Chapter 4
15. Hyginus *de munitionibus castrorum* 56–7; see Chapter 4
16. Davies and Jones 2006, 101–4
17. Welfare and Swan 1995, 43–4
18. Davies and Jones 2006, 135–8
19. Davies and Jones 2006, 15
20. Davies and Jones 2006, 118–20
21. Caesar *de Bello Gallico* VI.37
22. Vegetius *Epitoma* I.21
23. Hyginus *de munitionibus castrorum* 4; see Chapter 4
24. Josephus *Bellum Iudaicum* V.68–72; see Chapter 4
25. Davies and Jones 2006, 135–41
26. Welfare and Swan 1995, 96
27. Tacitus *Agricola* 20
28. Ammianus Marcellinus XXIV, 1, 3
29. See Davies 2006, 9–24
30. Vegetius *Epitoma* I, 21; see Chapter 4
31. Appian *Iberica* 86; Tacitus *Annals* XIII, 34-5; see Chapter 4
32. Vegetius *Epitoma* I.23
33. Milner 1996, 24n
34. Xenophon *The Education of Cyrus* VIII.5.3
35. Hyginus *de munitionibus castrorum* 56; see Chapter 4
36. Vegetius *Epitoma* I.23; Hyginus *de munitionibus castrorum* 56; see Chapter 4
37. Hyginus *de munitionibus castrorum* 56; see Chapter 8
38. For example, work on the pottery found along the Antonine Wall has identified north African cooking styles: Swan 1999
39. Bowman and Thomas 1991; 1994 and online at http://vindolanda.csad.ox.ac.uk/
40. For example, Roxan 1978; see Holder 1982, 104–133 for the garrison of Britain
41. Tacitus *Agricola* 35–7
42. Dobson 1981, 9; Breeze 1988, 8–10

43. Hanson 1991, 137
44. Mann 1985, 23; Breeze 1988, 9–10
45. Roy 1793, 52; see Chapter 6
46. Keppie 1984, 33
47. Hanson 1978, 142–3; Grillone 1977, xii, fig. 11; Lenoir 1979; Gilliver 1999, 87
48. Welfare and Swan 1995, 57–60
49. Roy 1793, 73–4
50. Richmond and McIntyre 1934, 55, fig. 1
51. Collingwood and Richmond 1969, 11
52. Gilliver 1999, 84–5
53. Maxwell 1982
54. Frere 1985a
55. See Salvatore 1996; Dobson 2008
56. Richmond 1962
57. Dilke 1971, 82–4
58. Maxwell 2004, 82–5
59. Richardson 2000, 431–2
60. Hanson and Maxwell 1986, 133–4; Breeze 2006a, 63–4
61. Tacitus *Agricola* 29–38; St Joseph 1978
62. Tacitus *Agricola* 29
63. Peddie 1987; Breeze 1988
64. Roy 1793; see Chapter 6
65. Reed 1976, 96
66. Herodian III.14.3; Cassius Dio LXXVI.13
67. Cassius Dio LXXVI. 11,2
68. Peddie 1987, 23–5, 180–4
69. For example, Peddie 1987, 27–32; Breeze 1988; Fulford 2000
70. Schlüter 1999; Wells 2003, 54–5
71. Hanson 2007
72. Breeze 1984a
73. Maxwell 2004
74. Breeze 1984b, 41
75. Tacitus *Agricola* 29–38

CHAPTER 6 – HISTORY OF ARCHAEOLOGICAL DISCOVERY

1. For example, there is a summary of accounts of Hadrian's Wall in Breeze 2006b
2. Price 1814, 168
3. Birley 1936, 69–73
4. Davies and Jones 2006, 187–94
5. Jones and Maxwell 2008
6. For example, Maitland 1757, 200; Gough's edition of Camden's *Britannia* 1790, iii, 414ff
7. Commissioned by the Duke of Cumberland after the battle of Culloden, between 1747 and 1755
8. Roy 1793; a further manuscript (the Kings Manuscript) is located in the British Library and was completed in July 1773
9. Jameson 1786, 16–18
10. Crawford 1949, 95–7
11. Jones forthcoming 2011, 141–2
12. Charlton and Day 1984; MacLauchlan 1857
13. MacLauchlan 1852, 26
14. Welfare and Swan 1995, 130
15. MacLauchlan 1857
16. For example, his *Topography of Roman Scotland North of the Antonine Wall*, published in 1949 (which was based on his Rhind Lectures to the Society of Antiquaries of Scotland in 1943)
17. St Joseph 1976, 2
18. Jones forthcoming 2011, 132–3
19. RCAHMW 1976; Davies and Jones 2006, 3
20. Steer and Feachem 1954, 81; RCAHMS 1957
21. Further details in Jones forthcoming 2011

22. Roy 1793, Pl. XII
23. Callander 1919, 138ff
24. Crawford 1949, 64
25. Cadw's 'Roman Fort Environs Project' – see Burnham and Davies (eds); Hadrian's Wall – see Breeze 2006b, 182, 246, 306. 333, 397

CHAPTER 7 – RE-USE AND SURVIVAL
1. Josephus *Bellum Iudaicum* III.90
2. Upstanding camps are known from such diverse locations around the Empire as Spain, the Netherlands, Romania, Egypt and Israel
3. Breeze 1984b, 37, 63; Roy 1793, Pl. XXXV
4. Josephus *Bellum Iudaicum* V.68–72
5. Davies and Jones 2006, 122–4
6. Welfare and Swan 1995, 77–9
7. RCAHMS 1956, 376; Jones forthcoming 2011, 293–4
8. Davies and Jones 2006, 95–8
9. Jones forthcoming 2011, 191–2
10. Jones forthcoming 2011, 179–80
11. Jones forthcoming 2011, 248–9
12. Davies and Jones 2006, 104
13. Frontinus *Strategemata* II.XI.7

CHAPTER 8 – FORM: DEFENCES, GATES AND ANNEXES
1. See Jones forthcoming 2011
2. Vegetius *Epitoma* I.24; III.8
3. Hyginus *de munitionibus castrorum*, 50
4. Welfare and Swan 1995, 17
5. Vegetius *Epitoma* III, 8
6. Vegetius *Epitoma* I, 24
7. Vegetius *Epitoma* I, 24; Hyginus *de munitionibus castrorum*, 50
8. Hyginus *de munitionibus castrorum*, 49
9. Welfare and Swan 1995, 57–60
10. See Gilliver 1993b
11. Livy XXXIII, 5; Vegetius *Epitoma* I.21, 24; III.8
12. Bennett 1982
13. Welfare and Swan 1995, 17, 36–8
14. Hyginus *de munitionibus castrorum* 48
15. Jones forthcoming 2011
16. Macdonald 1916, 332–5; Jones forthcoming 2011, 296–7
17. Hill 2006, 100
18. Hyginus *de munitionibus castrorum* 54
19. Caesar *de Bello Civili* III.67; Gilliver 1993b, 52–3; Bennett 1982, 204
20. Maxfield 1975, 144–7
21. Caesar *de Bello Gallico* VII.72–3
22. Jones 2005a
23. Vegetius *Epitoma* III.8
24. For comparative plans of all the camps in Britain, see Welfare and Swan 1995, fig. 6, Davies and Jones 2006, fig. 15, and Jones forthcoming 2011, fig. 47
25. Welfare and Swan 1995, 57–60, 34–6
26. Welfare and Swan 1995, 169 (Norton Fitzwarren), 67 (Newton on Trent)
27. Welfare and Swan 1995, 92–5 (Dargues), 44–50 (Troutbeck)
28. Jones forthcoming 2011, 288
29. Welfare and Swan 1995, 137–42
30. Jones forthcoming 2011, 278 (Milrighall); Philpott 1998 (Hoole)
31. Kennedy and Riley 1990, 107–8 (Jordan); Aharoni 1961; Lenoir 1977, 705 (Israel); Maxfield 2009, 70–3 (Egypt)
32. Maxwell 1989
33. Rodríguez Martín and Gorges 2006

34. Dobson 2008
35. Davies and Jones 2006, 178–85, 187–94
36. Dunwell and Keppie 1995; see Jones forthcoming 2011, 191–2
37. See Jones forthcoming 2011, 316–7
38. Hyginus *de munitionibus castrorum* 49–50, 55
39. Welfare and Swan 1995, 83–4 (Chapel Rig); 103–4 (Glenwhelt Leazes)
40. Stefan 1997
41. Welfare and Swan 1995, 75–7
42. Davies and Jones 2006, 169–73
43. Davies and Jones 2006, 170–1
44. Roy 1793, 65, Pl. XI
45. Rogers 1993, 286
46. Jones forthcoming 2011, 85–6, 179–80
47. Jones and McKeague 2009
48. See Jones forthcoming 2011
49. Jones forthcoming 2011, 285–6
50. Jones forthcoming 2011, 129–31
51. Caesar *de Bello Gallico* VIII.5
52. Frere 1985b
53. Raisen and Rees 1996: 40–1, 44
54. Strachan 1999
55. Hughes et al 1995; Welfare and Swan 1995, 150–3; Davies and Jones 2006, 34
56. Bailey 2000
57. Caesar *de Bello Gallico* VII.72–3
58. Johnston 1994, 258
59. The first volume of these extensive excavations has been published – see Cook and Dunbar 2008
60. Jones 2009a
61. Hyginus *de munitionibus castrorum* 2
62. Frere 1985b
63. Jones forthcoming 2011, 183–4
64. Davies and Jones 2006, 20, 103–4
65. Neighbour 1998
66. Welfare and Swan 1995, 41–2
67. Tacitus *Histories* iv.35
68. Austin and Rankov 1995, 191
69. Bowman and Thomas 1991
70. For example, Sallust *de Bello Jugurtha* XLIV–XLV for the former, Caesar *de Bello Gallico* VI.37 for the latter, although Caesar also suggests they were allowed within the camp defences – *de Bello Gallico* VI.36
71. Birley 2009, 139–40
72. Vegetius *Epitoma* I.21

CHAPTER 9 – DISTRIBUTION, CHRONOLOGY AND CONTEXT

1. For further discussion of aerial survey biases in Roman archaeology, see Jones 2005b
2. Tacitus *Annals* I.49; see Chapter 8
3. Described in Tacitus *Agricola* 25
4. Tacitus *Agricola* 24
5. Welfare and Swan 1995, 40
6. See Jones forthcoming 2011
7. See Jones forthcoming 2011
8. Tacitus *Agricola* 24
9. See Jones forthcoming 2011
10. Robertson 1980; Maxwell 1989
11. Tacitus *Agricola* 25
12. Tacitus *Agricola* 38
13. Vegetius *Epitoma* I.27; I.9
14. Cassius Dio LXXVI.13
15. Excavations in 2007 were by David Woolliscroft and Birgitta Hoffmann from the Roman Gask project (http://www.theromangaskproject.org.uk/)

16. See Jones forthcoming 2011
17. Excavations by R. J. F. Jones and Bradford University.
18. Jones forthcoming 2011, 282–4
19. Breeze 1984a, 268
20. Welfare and Swan 1995, 85–90; Richmond and Keeney 1937
21. See Jones forthcoming 2011
22. Welfare and Swan 1995, 57–60 (Rey Cross), 34–6 (Crackenthorpe), 43–4 (Plumpton Head)
23. Cow Close was discovered from the air in 2006: Gates and Ainsworth 2008
24. Caruana 1992, 101–3
25. Maxwell 1981, 39
26. For example, see Davies and Jones 2006, 54–66
27. Welfare and Swan 1995, 164–5 (Uffington), 166–8 (Whittington); Davies and Jones 2006, 104–7 (Pen Plaenau), 108–9 (Penrhos)
28. Reddé 1995
29. For example, in Spain at Peñarredonda: Morillo 2003; in Egypt at Qasr Ibrim: Maxfield 2009, 70–3
30. Richmond 1962
31. Aharoni 1961, 161-2; Lenoir 1977, 715
32. Cassius Dio LXIX.13.2
33. For a more detailed discussion of camps with *claviculae*, see Jones 2009b
34. Gilliver 1993a; Hyginus *de munitionibus castrorum* 49–55
35. Davies and Jones 2006, 67–90
36. Davies and Jones 2006, 88; Burnham and Davies (eds) 2010
37. Welfare and Swan 1995, 24
38. Richmond 1932, 76 and information from Dr P. Wilson, English Heritage
39. Ogilvie and Richmond 1967, 62–3
40. Tacitus *Agricola* 25
41. Tacitus *Agricola* 20
42. Roy 1793, 65, Pl. XI
43. See Chapter 3 and earlier in this chapter
44. Tipping 1997, 25
45. Jones 2009a; Hodgson 2009

CHAPTER 10 – CONCLUSIONS

1. Tacitus *Annals* XII.33
2. See Davies and Jones 2006, 88–90 for a fuller discussion of the evidence
3. Tacitus *Agricola* 28
4. Tacitus *Agricola* 35
5. Tacitus *Agricola* 26
6. Cook and Dunbar 2008
7. Austin & Rankov 1995, 116

Index

forts, Roman, 9, 10, 14, 16, 17, 18, 20, 24, 25, 27, 28, 29, 30, 31, 32, 40, 41, 46, 48, 55, 56, 57, 59, 63, 66, 68, 69, 70, 76, 77, 81, 83, 85, 87, 88, 91, 93, 94, 95, 96, 99, 100, 104, 105, 106, 107, 108, 109, 111, 115, 118, 120, 123, 126, 128, 129, 130, 131, 133, 134, 135, *figs. 19, 32, 34, 44, 51, 52, 58, 64, 66 & 71, col. pls. 20 & 21*

forum (market), 33, 35, 37, 123, 137, *fig. 14*

Four Laws, *see* Swine Hill

frontier, Roman, 9, 10, 17, 24, 25, 27, 34, 48, 105, 109, 133, *also see* Antonine Wall, German *Limes* & Hadrian's Wall

Frontinus, *see* Julius Frontinus

Gallaberry, camp (Dumfriesshire), 64, 86, *fig. 30*

Galley Gill, camp (Cumbria), 81, 136

gates (entrances), of camps, 12, 18, 20, 22, 23, 27, 28, 29, 32, 39, 43, 45, 46, 49, 62, 63, 64, 65, 71, 72, 73, 76, 77, 79, 81, 83, 86–94, 98, 100, 101, 102, 103, 105, 112, 114, 115, 116, 118, 120, 121–8, 131, 132, 136, 137, 138, *figs. 5, 33, 46, 47, 48, 49 & 70, col. pls. 13 & 15*

clavicula/claviculae, 63, 87–94, 105, 118–20, 121, 123, 126, 127, 131, 137, 138, *figs. 15, 46, 48, 69, col. pl. 13*

cuspate, 87, 123, *fig. 46*

porta decumana, 39, 40, 41, 45, 46, 138, *fig. 14*

porta praetoria, 40, 45, 86, 102, *fig. 14*

porta principalis dextra, 39, 138, *fig. 14*

porta principalis sinistra, 39, 138, *fig. 14*

Stracathro-type, 65, 87, 91–4, 126, 127–8, 132, 138, *figs. 46, 47, 48, 51, 70, 71, col. pls. 14, 15*

titulus/tituli, 20–2, 29, 43, 62, 63, 72, 87–91, 103, 105, 112, 114, 115, 116, 118, 120, 121, 123, 128, 138, *figs. 15, 33, 35, 46, 48 & 49*

gathering ground, 126

Gaul (France), 13, 35, 95, 97–9

Gelligaer Common, camps (Glamorgan), 91, *fig. 50*

geophysical survey, 68–9, 89, 100, 102, 134, 136

German *Limes*, 10

Germanicus, general, 31, 106

Girvan Mains, camps (Ayrshire), 108

glandes (sling bullets), 23, 137

glass, Roman, 108

Glenlochar, camps (Dumfries & Galloway), 96, 100, 104, *fig. 55*

Glenwhelt Leazes, camp (Northumberland), 63, 90

Gosbecks Farm (Essex), 106

Grampian Mountains, 15, 61

Grassy Walls, camp (Perthshire), 67, 112, *figs. 33 & 60*

Gratian, Emperor, 34

Great Chesters, fort (Northumberland), 81, *fig. 42*

Greeks, people, 32, 33

groma, 32, 33, 137, col. pl. 6

grübenhäuser, 76, 137

Hadrian, Emperor, 16, 34, 89, 123, 127

Hadrianic period, 25, 89, 104, 116, 123, 127

Hadrian's Wall, frontier & camps, 10, 16, 17, 20, 24, 29, 42, 48, 59, 63, 68, 69, 81, 84, 90, 101, 104, 105, 108, 109, 118, 123, 132, 133, 134, 135, *fig. 42, col. pl. 9*

Haltwhistle Burn, camps (Northumberland), 59

Hill of Gourdie, quarry (Perthshire), 27

hill-fort, 14, 20, 23, 24, 89, 90, 131, 138, *figs. 4, 6*

Hillside Annan, camp (Dumfriesshire), 95, 108

Hillside Dunblane, camp (Stirlingshire), 80

Hindwell Farm, camps (Radnorshire), 40, 41, 42, 69, 70, *col. pl. 8*

history/histories (Roman), 11, 33, 35, 36, *fig. 14*

Hittites, people, 32

hoard, coin, 17

holding ground, 11, 47–58

Hoole, camp (Cheshire), 87

horses, 18, 38, 53, 56, 94, 98, 100, 105, 135

hostages, 39, 104, 105

Household Dunipace, camp (Stirlingshire), 66–7, *fig. 60*

Hungary, 30, 127

Hyginus, author, 34, 38, 39, 40, 41, 43, 45, 46, 48, 49, 50–2, 55, 57, 80, 81, 83, 86, 90, 100, 123, *fig. 15*

impedimenta, *see* baggage,

Inchtuthil, fort & camps (Perthshire), 27, 50, 94, 95, 96, 98, 100, 129, *figs. 21, 54 & 73*

Innerpeffray East & West, camps (Perthshire), 85–6, 115, *figs. 56, 60 & 61*

intaglio, Roman, 118

internal features, *see* oven, pit,

invasion, Roman, 13, 14, 23, 46, 55, 106, 108, 131, 132, 133, *also see* Claudian invasion

Invergowrie, camp (Perthshire), 67

Inverness, 15

Ireland, 108

Irish Sea, 108

Iron Age, 13, 15, 17, 20, 41, 58, 85, 96, 104–5, 131, 133

Isca Dumnoniorum, *see* Exeter

Israel, 10, 20, 23, 51, 87, 94, 123, 127, *fig. 1*

itineraries, 24, 115, 134

iugerum, unit of measurement, 52, 138

Jameson, Revd, antiquarian, 62

Jerusalem, city (Israel), 42, 71

Jones, Theophilus, antiquarian, 59

Josephus, historian, 20, 35, 42, 43, 59, 70, 71

Judaea, 123

Jugurthine War, 35

Julian, Emperor, 43

Julius Agricola, governor, 9, 14–15, 20, 33, 35, 36, 42–3, 48, 53, 54, 55, 57, 58, 60, 63, 107–8, 109, 126, 127, 132

Julius Caesar, 13, 20, 23, 35, 37, 41, 83, 95, 96, 99, 106, 107, 121–3, 131, 138

Julius Frontinus, governor, 14, 32, 33, 34, 78, 132

Julius Severus, governor, 123

Kair House, camp (Aberdeenshire), 112, *fig. 60*

Kalkriese, battlefield (Germany), 55

Keithock, camp (Angus), 74, 133, *fig. 56*

Kent, 13, 14, 106

Kintore, camp (Aberdeenshire), 12, 34, 55, 57, 58, 73–4, 95, 96, 98–100, 105, 116, 117, 130, 134, 135, 136, *figs. 53 & 63*

Kirkbuddo, camp (Angus), 74, *figs. 37 & 56, col. pl. 10*

Kirkpatrick-Fleming, camps (Dumfriesshire), 116, *fig. 62*

Knockcross, camp (Cumbria), 108

Lantonside, fortlet (Dumfriesshire), 108

latera praetorii, 39, 138

layout of camps, 11, 18, 32, 33, 37–45, 51, 71, 86, 98, 116, 127, 130, 135, *figs. 14, 15 & 20*

leather tents, Roman, 18, 94, 95, 105, *also see* tents

legions, 9, 15, 33, 37, 41, 42, 45, 48, 49, 51, 52, 54, 56, 57, 75, 107, 127, 137, 138

Legio II Adiutrix, 48, 127

Legio II Augusta, 14, 48, 107

Legio II Parthica, 54,

Legio VI Victrix, 49

Legio IX Hispana, 48, 127, 132

Legio X Fretensis, 51

Legio XX Valeria Victrix, 48

Leighton, fort (Shropshire), 30

Light Detection & Ranging (LiDAR), 68, *col. pl. 9*

lilia, 83, 84, 96, 138

lime-kilns, 27, 94

Lincoln, fortress, 127

Lintrose, camp (Perthshire), 74, *fig. 56*

literary sources, 10, 14, 15, 17, 24, 31, 34, 36, 45, 47, 59, 106, 131, 132

Little Kerse, camp (Stirlingshire), 104, 133, *fig. 7*

Livy, historian (Titus Livius), 32, 35, 81

lixae, *see* camp followers

Llandrindod Common, camps (Radnorshire), 29, 59, 60, *fig. 25*

Llanfor, fort & camp (Merioneth), 69, *fig. 34*

Llanymynech Hill (Montgomery/Shropshire), 20

Llyn Hiraethlyn, camp (Merioneth), 28, *fig. 11*

Loch Ryan, 108

Lochlands, camps (Stirlingshire), 30, 82, 89, 96, *fig. 7*

Logie Durno, camp (Aberdeenshire), 15, 52, 54, 116, 117, *figs. 22 & 63*

Longforgan, camp (Angus), 102, 103, *fig. 56*

Machaerus, siege (Jordan), 20
MacLauchlan, Henry, antiquarian, 63
Maitland, William, antiquarian, 67
Map of Roman Britain, 8, 64
Marcomanni, people, 35
Marcus, camp (Angus), 103, *figs. 56 & 57*
Marcus Aurelius, Emperor, 34
Masada, siege camps (Israel), 10, 20, 51, 52, 53, 94, 123, *fig. 1*
Mauchamp, camp (France), 121
Maurice, Byzantine Emperor, 35
Maxwell, Gordon S., archaeologist, 50, 52, 67
McIntyre, James, archaeologist, 49, 50, *fig. 20*
Medieval period, 115, *also see* early Medieval, Post Medieval
Melville, Robert, antiquarian, 60, 61, 62, 74
Melville Nurseries, pits (Midlothian), 96
metalworking, Roman, 99–100, 135
Metellus, consul, 35, 37, 38
Milestone House, camp (Northumberland), 85
military manual, 11, 33, 34, 38, 40, 41, 47, 48, 123
Military Survey of Scotland, 61
Milrighall, camp (Scottish Borders), 87
Milton, fort (Dumfriesshire), 128
Mona, *see* Anglesey
Mons Graupius, battle of, 9, 15, 48, 52, 53, 55, 57, 58, 60, 132
Montrose Basin, 108
Moss Side, camp (Cumbria), 98, 100, 104
mules, 37, 49, 53, 55, 56, 57, 80, 94, 98, 135
Muirhouses, camp (West Lothian), 77, *figs 7, 40*

Nahal Hever, camps (Israel), 23, 87, 123, 127
Newstead, fort & camps (Scottish Borders), 118, *figs. 64, 65, col. pl. 21, front cover*
Neolithic period, 13, 64
Netherlands, 10, 88, 104, 127
Newton on Trent, camp (Lincolnshire), 87
Nith, River, 90, 108
Normandykes, camp (Aberdeenshire), 75, 76, 95, *figs. 38 & 63*
North Channel, 108
Norton Fitzwarren, camp (Somerset), 87
Novantae, people, 20
Numantia, siege camps (Spain), 10, 20, 33, 37, 51, 88, 121, *col. pl. 3*

Oakwood, camp (Selkirkshire, Scottish Borders), 66, 87, *fig. 32*
officers, 18, 43, 99, 127, *also see* camp prefect, centurions, *quaestor*, *praetorium*, tribunes
Onasander, philosopher, 35, 40
Ordnance Survey, 8, 20, 61, 63, 64, 67, *fig. 43*
Ordovices, people, 14, 33, 131
orientation of camps, 11, 45–7
Orkney, 15

Ostorius Scapula, governor, 14
ovens, 12, 58, 69, 79, 94–101, 105, 130, 134, 135, 136, *fig. 53, col. pl. 17 & 18*

palisade, 31, 32, 79, 81, 83, 106, 131, 136, *col. pl. 11, front cover*
Paternus, lawyer & soldier, 34
Pen Plaenau, camp (Denbighshire), 121, *fig. 68*
Peña Redonda, camp (Numantia, Spain), *col. pl. 3*
Pennymuir, camps (Scottish Borders), 71, 72, 134, *fig. 35, back cover*
Penrhos, camp (Denbighshire), 121, *fig. 67*
Pentaur, poem of, 32
Persian Expedition, 43
Persians, people, 32
Perth, 17, 133
Petillius Cerealis, governor, 14, 120
Picts/Pictish, people, 15, 17, 34
pila muralia/pilum murale, 81, 138, *fig. 42*
pits, 10, 12, 30, 34, 50, 58, 76, 79, 83, 84, 93, 94–101, 104, 105, 130, 134, 136, *figs. 44, 54 & 55*, also see lilia
Plumpton Head, camp (Cumbria), 40, 85, 120
Plutarch, biographer, 32
Polybius, historian, 33, 35, 37, 42, 48, 49, 51, 57, *fig. 14*
Post Medieval period, 20
pottery, 10, 24, 25, 34, 89, 94, 99, 100, 104, 108, 111, 116, 120, 133, 134, 135
    amphora, 15
    beaker, 34, 134
    coarse ware, 111
    mortaria, 111
praefectus castrorum, *see* camp prefect
praetentura, 39, 138
Praetorian Guard, 34, 54
praetorium, 18, 37, 39, 45, 49, 138
Price, Revd Thomas, antiquarian, 59, 60, *fig. 25*
Pseudo-Hyginus, *see* Hyginus
Publius Quinctilius Varus, general, 15, 56
Pyrrhus, King of Epirus, 32

Qadesh/Kadesh, Hittite city (Syria), 32
Qasr Ibrim, camp (Egypt), 87
quaestor, 37, 39, 138
Quintus Veranius, governor, 35

radiocarbon dating, 55, 96, 98, 110, 116
Raeburnfoot, fort & camp (Dumfriesshire), 93, *fig. 52, col. pl. 15*
Raedykes, camp (Aberdeenshire), 74, 82, 85, 116, *figs. 43 & 63*
Ramesses II, Egyptian Pharaoh, 32
ramparts (banks), of camps, 9, 18, 22, 23, 24, 28, 31, 37, 38, 40, 43, 45, 52, 62, 63, 70–6, 79–82, 87, 90, 91, 93, 94, 95, 98, 101, 104, 105, 106, 111, 121, 131, 132, 136, 137, 138, *fig. 41, col. pls. 10 & 11, front cover*
redoubt, Civil War, 20
remote sensing, 12, 68–9, 79, 107

Renieblas, camp (Spain), 51
re-use of camps, 12, 25, 46, 70–4, 76, 118, 120, 130, 133, 134
Rey Cross, camp (County Durham), 49, 50, 81, 86, 120, 134, *fig. 20*
Retentura, 39, 45, 138, *fig. 15*
Rhine, River, 10
Richborough, fort (Kent), 14, 106
Richmond, Sir Ian, archaeologist, 49, 50, *figs 1 & 20*
Risingham, fort (Northumberland), 63
roads, Roman, 16, 24, 27, 28, 29, 30, 46, 49, 63, 64, 71, 75, 77, 78, 85, 106, 107, 108, 110, 111, 115, 117, 118, 120, 134
    Dere Street, 46, 63, 71, 85, 117, 118, 134
    Sarn Helen, 75
    Stainmore Pass, 120
    Stanegate, 16
    Watling Street, 63
roads, within fortifications,
    intervallum, 39, 49, 52, 95, 98, 137, *figs 14 & 15*
    streets, 32, 33, 49, 50, 71, 95, 100, 111
    via quintana, 39, 138, *figs. 14 & 15*
    via praetoria, 138, *fig. 15*
    via principalis, 39, 45, 138, figs. 14 & 15
    via sagularis, 39, 138
Roman Empire, 9, 10, 14, 16, 18, 19, 20, 32, 33, 34, 35, 37, 45, 53, 55, 70, 87, 88, 89, 94, 109, 117, 118, 121, 123, 134, 136, *col. pl. 1*
Roman Republic, 9, 32, 33, 35, 37, 51, 123
Romania, 10, 16, 88, 90, 123, 127
Rome (Italy), 9, 14, 15, 16, 17, 33, 35, 105, 123, 133, *col. pl. 7*
Roy, General William, antiquarian, 33, 35, 48, 49, 50, 54, 58, 61, 62, 67, 74, 85, 91, 127, *figs. 26 & 51*
Royal Air Force, 64, *fig. 32*
Royal Commission on the Ancient & Historical Monuments of Scotland (RCAHMS), 66
Royal Commission on the Ancient & Historical Monuments of Wales (RCAHMW), 66
Royal Corps of Military Surveyors & Draftsmen, 35
Royal Flying Corps, 64
Royal Society, 61

Saalburg, fort (Germany), *col. pl. 17*
Salisbury Plain (Wiltshire), 28, 131
Sallust, historian, 33
Sarmatians, people, 35
Saxon Shore Fort, 109
Scipio Africanus the Younger, general, 28, 37, 38, 45
Scots, people, 34
scouts, 19, 50, 104, 130, 135, 137
Second World War, 64, 65
Septimius Severus, Emperor, 17, 24, 34, 54, 55, 108, 109, 112, 118, 133, 134
Serbia, 127
settlements, prehistoric, 13, 15, 17, 20, 23, 24, 31, 104, 138